THE KALEIDOSCOPE OF LIFE:

Essays on Identity and Indigenous Knowledge Systems.

Sithembele Isaac Xhegwana

Mwanaka Media and Publishing Pvt Ltd,
Chitungwiza Zimbabwe
*
Creativity, Wisdom and Beauty

Publisher: *Mmap*
Mwanaka Media and Publishing Pvt Ltd
24 Svosve Road, Zengeza 1
Chitungwiza Zimbabwe
mwanaka@yahoo.com
mwanaka13@gmail.com
www.africanbookscollective.com/publishers/mwanaka-media-and-publishing
https://facebook.com/MwanakaMediaAndPublishing/

Distributed in and outside N. America by African Books Collective
orders@africanbookscollective.com
www.africanbookscollective.com

ISBN: 978-1-77928-534-8
EAN: 9781779285348

DISCLAIMER
All views expressed in this publication are those of the author
and do not necessarily reflect the views of *Mmap*.

TABLE OF CONTENTS

INTRODUCTION

The arrival of Portuguese adventurers, led by Vasco da Gama, marked the beginning of one of the many notorious invasions that changed the fate of not only Africa but also that of developing nations. After a lengthy sea journey heading East, da Gama landed 'unexpectedly' on February 3, 1488, near the stormy seaside at the Cape. He then continued to Malindi, Kenya, where the Sultan (another invader) allowed him to plant a pillar, build a chapel, and set a trading post. From there on his journey of 'amicable trade' with the 'natives', he Christened the largely amassed geographic amalgamation he encountered. The simple gesture of erecting crosses was some form of cartography whose meaning did not fall short of an early rebut of colonialism.

Da Gama, suspicious of the sentiments of the sometimes uncomfortable prime owners of both the land and livestock he sought to steal, lacking a better word, carried on (like many of his predecessors) with the journey to discover a route to the most elusive East. Almost two centuries later, the Cape found itself as a 'refreshment station' for a group led by no other than Jan van Riebeck who also was following in the footsteps of his many Western predecessors. The only thing that set him apart was, in the disguise of establishing a refreshment station, together with his entourage, a decision to be a permanent resident of the then Cape. This of course would be at the expense of the Cape's historical known prime inhabitants; the Khoisan and the amaXhosa.

At this time and age, we all are aware of this plunder which did not only end with natural resources, livestock and people who were either turned into slaves and also ravished; the indigenous knowledge systems were either appropriated or completely destroyed. The Western epistemology, in the form of religion and education, found the 'natives' not only left indigent but almost reduced to nothing. After they had been stripped of everything they had, in the form of both the infrastructure and cosmology, mostly practiced in the form of specialized artwork and supernatural invocations, different forms of Western inculturation were implanted.

At this time and age, we all are aware of this plunder which did not end with natural resources, livestock, and people who were domesticated and shipped to the West as slaves; it continued in the form of appropriation and destruction of our indigenous knowledge systems. Our primary knowledge, conveyed from one generation to the next through our languages, took a direct hit when our languages were criminalized. Africans had to speak in the master's language! A look at the national languages in African states bears the legacy of the colonizers. What is disturbing is that the plunder continues.

Though mostly based in the historical and spiritual life of the present day amaXhosa people, this collection of essays has a common thread; lifting up the veil covering the present-day Western ideology in the context of South Africa and Africa in large. In the present day period of time where it is being encouraged that these kinds of veils should be vilified under the banner of decolonialization, Xhegwana's voice seeks clarity. As he has so excellently done in his different volumes of poetry collections, he is still continuing with his decolonial input.

The author himself, having been a victim of this furious but passive inculturation engages the silent harbingers of this epistemology and thus deliberate lies about Africa. Today, Africa needs to not only to lift the veil but to rip it off in its quest for decolonialization. Xhegwana's voice, in its own ways and manners, emulates and thus adds to the clarion call of decentering from Western knowledge/s; that of Sol Plaatjie, S.E.K. Mqhayi, Mongane Wally Serote, Ngugi wa Thiong'o, Captain Ibrahim Traore, and many other heroes stirring the African renaissance.

Andrew Maina.

Founder of Kendeka Prize for African Literature.

STARTING FROM MY PLACE: NOTES ON AN AESTHETIC[1]

The sun rising from the west? Is this a trick my mind is playing on me? Or is it an after-effect of all *meaningful* journeys? The real purpose of Homer's *Odyssey*, I think, expresses itself when Odysseus descends to the Greek underworld. The quite familiar character of the Theban prophet (like Job in the Hebrew Bible?) had done the most impossible, overcoming the horrible darkness of the underworld, when others could only sink in its overwhelming presence. Throughout the *Odyssey*, the Greek mind muses about its origin and that of human kind, as gathered from their mythology. To my mind, its most explicit thesis – beyond propagating the cult of the master race, to the favor of ancient Greece – is that of the human spirit's ability to prosper, through an act of will, even against what Joseph Conrad has rightly called the destructive element.

Everything becomes clear after this visit; Odysseus meeting his dead mother and knowing everything that lies ahead. From now onwards both reader and protagonist share the dividends. Against all odds, Odysseus does not mind his many detours. Which to me could be the only reason why Ezra Pound opens his *Cantos* (also a cultural & spiritual

---

[1] A summarized and updated version of this essay was published by the English Academy Review, March 2023.

odyssey) with a translation of that most defining journey –
the descend to the underworld.

II

The bus shivers, and then it moves. Lost in the dark night.
Lost in the journey, the draining journey. The palm trees,
scattered alongside the Cape Metro Rail, swaying along the
road taking us away from Cape Town; somewhere along the
way they disappear. The street lamps, bending their necks,
scrutinize us. On a dusty field, just across the road,
motorbike riders attract my attention. Blinking billboards,
electronic advertisements swooping routinely. Tall long-
trimmed trees – I wish I knew what they are called. A power
station; dams both for supplier and human waste purposes.
Two tall palm trees overseeing posh houses just across the
road.

The Tygerberg hills, the mountains again. For the first time,
I become aware that Cape Town is like an island,
surrounded by mountains. Without notice, the bus
assistants make their announcements again. Wouldn't it be
better if they just played recordings? (The computerized
voices could do the job much better). I suppose it has all to
do with the personal touch of the marketing beast. Houses
like mushrooms sprouting on the Cape sands – that is all I
can see. PPC cement plants, statues, burial stones and
Stellenbosch farms.

Empty, bare and clean soil for the first time. It ushers in that
bareness and nakedness around me. The ancient earth that

we can easily forget in town is still around. Lately, we have become too much used to the wide concrete slabs that cover every corner of the human-made world. My mind cannot help but go back to the primordial cultures now extinct or marginalized: that of the Bushmen; that of the native African; and that of the trees and nature that have fallen victim to our human progress. Though funded by a selfish capitalist or liberal agenda, it is only now I can appreciate the far-reaching sight of Cecil John Rhodes, who at the summit of his economic power gave orders for a piece of ground to be preserved from human progress, the Rondebosch Common. Every time I see this piece of ground, I am reminded of how powerful the voices of the dead are in any community, setting aside their socio-economic status which I could say still protects Rhodes' will. However, the obstinacy of recent international social movements like #Rhodes Must Fall fly right in the face of my preceding statement.

I wonder if lately I could lay claim to the wisdom whose custodian has always been the indigenous knowledge systems laid bare in the preceding paragraph. I long abandoned it in search of what I conceived to be a higher order, unfortunately closely intertwined with the white man's interpretation of being.

An old palm tree standing alone with only the blue skies just over its sullen head. A crescent moon stabs the silent skies. To me, the sign stands like a bow wedged within the solid sheath of the skies. By the way, this moon is standing over what I assume to be the long-term territory of the pre-colonial Khoisan, one of our oldest and complicated civilisations. Under toil and savagery, they marched out of this territory to the edges of the Southern African landscape, into dry hot deserts. Yet, they left their art behind. The bus stops, it is refreshment time. An old man is surprised to see one of our fellow travelers, a young female university student from the University of Cape Town, smoking. This no longer catches people like me by surprise, I am used to witnessing different characters from different backgrounds asserting themselves through many forms of adolescent rebellion.

And now, again the bus stops at the middle of nowhere. The white mist is very dense and moves like a pregnant woman among the colonial gum trees. In this part of the world, the Xhosa-speaking Eastern Cape, a mist is an agent of evil. It heralds or crawls behind death. Here it is understood as an agent of evil spirits and is thought to be incarnated in figures of witches. Maybe I have just been ushered into my own *underworld*. Remember, the Greek underworld as presented by Homer also defies logic. It exists parallel to the present *cosmos*. To Homer, only a natural and physical landmark separates from this geographic location. Indeed, in every way this part of the world, the Eastern Cape, which is also where my natural home is, qualifies as a no-man's-land.

Like Robert Frost, I am now digging directly from the land to feed my art of poetry. One could say, like a cow or a bull of sacrifice, I am grazing. From the landscape itself, stories erupt like volcanoes; they demand one's attention. What else can one do but write? In the process, the inevitable happens: the discovery of the self. Jeremy Cronin's manifesto still looms high in our poetical landscape:

> *To learn how to speak*
> *With the voices of the land…*
> *To write a poem with words like:*
> *I am telling you*
> *Stompie, stickfast, golovan…*
> *To understand least inflections,*
> *To voice without swallowing*
> *Syllables born in tin shacks, or catch*
> *The 5.15 ikwata bust fife*
> *Chwannisberg train[2]*

Athough Cronin was definitely writing from a different experience and place to mine, I find that ironically there is a lot I identify with in his sentiments. Having been detached from my own amaXhosa community for a long period of time due to an acute religious encounter, an experience that resulted in a kind of 'exile', I am more of an outsider than perhaps Cronin could have been in these instances of foreign language worlds that he desired to capture in his poetry. Also, discovering that there is actually nothing I can do to reverse the experience, I have had to struggle to learn

---

[2] Cronin, J. 1983. <u>Inside</u>, Johannesburg: Ravan Press.

to be part of my formative world once more, even if only in the realms of imagination.

A few observations as we go along: white men close to nature and all its inherent benefits; horses peacefully grazing. A horse is just one of the many colonial figures that have adopted very well to the indigenous African context, while serving the master's purpose, both White and amaXhosa. The housing testifies to the unequal distribution of income that is common not only in the area but in South Africa as a whole. The ANC government driven projects can never change things even in hundred years to come. This indelible truth hits at us once we impartially observe the awful condition of the Eastern Cape villages.

Poverty; political motivated promises; a search for eternal votes and lack of understanding of the term constituency from both voter and politician. From this scenario one can safely exclude the former Transkei villages where the ANC government has successfully managed to bring government sponsored projects. These projects only serve as a veneer on the surface of the collective reality (that of poverty and unemployment) so that the political investors can reap the benefits (votes) in this very much competitive political environment. In this scenario of non-delivery at the other side of the Kei River where the ruling party does not perceive any threat, how does one explain the fact voters still choose the party anyway? What does one get from loyalty anyway? Abuse. Perpetual abuse. Neglect, even by those who are supposed to be your very messiahs, or who portray themselves as such.

The battle between the Matanzima royal brothers and Dr Lennox Sebe is far from being over. The new regime may want to obliterate individual memories in a desire to forge a new collective identity not only in these former homelands but also at a national level. How, in the face of everything, can one pretend that human beings can be or are machines? One can never program the human mind at will – that only exists in the realm of science fiction. How can reasonable human beings, old and young, men and women, forget such tribal atrocities that were committed in front of their very eyes for many decades? They may forgive, yes. But, begging for amnesia is asking for too much.

I occasionally get sick – mentally. And now I feel I am. The reality is that at times I am more paranoid than sick. I fear that one powerful voice may decide that it is no longer healthy for me to stand alone, speaking out. No doubt democracy, on its own a carefully crafted ideology, hardly caters for such individuals. Indeed, *every man stands alone. Next to him is the whirlwind.*

Here is the sea, earnest in its rumbling. I feel refreshed, able to start over again. Some observations: sailing ships; rocks stand guard between the sea and the national road. The bus television competes with my natural theology. The bus stops again, in the middle of nowhere. More observations: another gravel road runs away to Kenton-On-Sea; dry mimosa trees along the road and some red soil. This looks like the motherland, with Grahamstown making its presence felt. Do you want some myth-making? Here it is. Since the 1819 Makhanda revolution the land decided to be red. Due to the blood of the many Xhosa warriors slaughtered at the hands of technologically advanced English army, the local soil was anguished. This curse will be removed only if all the perpetrators (both Makhanda's men and the English army) perform a cleansing ritual – a thing they will never do. Why? They are all dead by now.

We stop at Kimberley Hall at Rhodes University. A completely English white world and all its advantages in the heart of this no-man's-land: this has always been a striking paradox to me. Hardly five kilometers from the small Victorian city, one sees mud houses also claiming their space along the Dr Jacob Zuma regional road. Just at the other side of the road one again sees very beautiful houses. It seems that these sharp contradictions have somehow managed to co-exist, third world and first world realities in parallel.

A beautiful and sad story. Beautiful because it speaks loudly of the resilience of these people even against the ravishing beauty of the advanced world. As if nothing is wrong with their state of being, they find reason for life to go on. But sad because one can never really figure out in one's mind how modern society seem to thrive best in contradictions. It is so striking that this combination of worst and best has a tendency of repeating itself throughout the South African landscape. I revisit an old theme, the dialectic of evil and good.

III

Like a rebellious child denying his heritage, it seems to be the duty of the modern writer to break away from his past. I am personally not sure about that. It becomes an even more complicated matter when it comes to African writers. Can one be taken seriously if one jumps to a 'European encounter' instead of probing one's 'African roots'? I am personally divided on this issue. If the complicated incidence of me being born in the Eastern Cape, a province in South Africa, forces me to root my imagination in the same geographical area, I must take up that challenge. If then, having taken up such an onerous task (of seeking to integrate myself, my consciousness and my awareness into my imagination) automatically denies me access to 'European encounter', the same encounter which happens to be part of my everyday experience (my hybrid Christianity and my missionary education for that matter), I will say "no!" to that.

Above all, one must be reminded that I hold the dubious prestige of being the first member of my matriarchal line of family to hold a higher European education. I have personally chosen to make an emphasis on "higher" because of my mother's Bantustan State "Royal Education" (that was very high and classic for its times) from Methodist missionaries in Mount Coke Hospital while she was under their custodianship for many years due to polio related complications. Although she went up to the upper echelons of what was on offer then, she unfortunately could not amalgamate her achievements because of the simple refusal of her mother to do so. Her elder brother, a mine worker then, had put aside money for her to be sent out to those Bantustan higher education or nursing colleges of the time. Instead, my grandmother used the money to build a house. Again, one of my grandmother's cousins offered to sponsor my mother's education in return that on her home-coming she should re-pay the loan in one way or another. Again, my most erstwhile grandmother refused such gestures! In much anger and defiance, my mother decided to join the village work force of domestic workers in King William's town where she faithfully served different masters until her retirement in 1984 after she gave birth to one of my sisters.

A personal note, I have just noted that during this specific calendar year, 2021 , I have reached Wole Soyinka's magic figure of 49. Another note; Soyinka's year of formal exile from his home country – 1994 – marks another year in my life; the arrival of a beast that has tormented my life for the past 27 years; bi-polar mood disorder (so Freud's descendants and grand children have termed it). From an African perspective; at least, this year marks the consolidation and arrival of my many vocations: poet, missionary, writer, African priest, traditional surgeon, etc). The calendar year 1994 also marks my many moments when I literally walked back from the journey of death. The angel of death must be tired now, please leave me alone! This makes me remember the most elusive fact that this illustrative African writer escaped an absentia life sentence from his home country! The honour that post-colonial African states bestow on their multi-coloured robed sons! Remember, Soyinka was the first African writer to be bestowed with a Nobel Prize in Literature.

The magic figure 49 also represents a very distinctive year in my literary career; when my name formally entered the terrain of African literature as I for the first time got published in the Best "New" African Poetry Anthology. Yes, it is almost 18 years since my first anthology *Scatter The Shrilling Bones* simultaneously saw the light of day and was also buried by socio-economic politics of African publishing. Not forgetting my debut work of 1991 *The Faint-Hearted Man* longlisted for the Noma Award for Publishing in Africa but suddenly disappeared in the global vulture machines of the recycling of literary works by international internet based giants at the expense of poor writers who get not even a penny as their work is being sold all over the world in different disguises. Also, many other creative achievements like being published in the *Sol Plaatjie European Union Poetry* Anthology. Having long not associated my creative work with financial gain, being listed among Africa's best, and those from the diaspora, is like a silent whisper from the Muse herself.

A most recent work, "Land of Thorns", a collaboration between my thirteen year old daughter has been another august literary achievement for me. It is in this anthology that through one of the poems, "Scattered Feathers" I attempt to recover the absence of my dear second wife, who sleeps distantly from me in a lonely grave in Corhana, an Eastern Cape semi-village somewhere close to Mthatha. Not even able to attend her funeral, forget about the honor to bury her, due to some squabbles that were prevailing between me and my in-laws, the Harmattan season of dry air that I always imagine, taste, and feel when I always think of her will take time to exit so the wet springs and summers we spent together may repossess me once more. As some means to achieve a state of eternal solace, I could only design a surrogate memorial service and erect a stone in her honor.

IV

A day before this trip, I am sitting on the steps of Jameson Hall, recently named Sarah Baartman Hall, at the University of Cape Town, staring at the red roofs – silhouettes of what's left – of the 17th century Cape Dutch world. As usual, I hope to get a reward from this occupation: a poem that could really convert what I see and feel into words. Unfortunately, this never seems to happen. My cell phone rings. I check the screen, a Vodacom number. That is my wife. Who else would phone me this time of the day? She really benefits from Vodacom's community outreach programs: the blue containers sheltering the public cell phones in King William's Town. She tells me she is depositing money in the bank for me to take a Greyhound bus the same night. *There is a crucial meeting we have to attend*, she stresses.

I am reluctant; I am so tired of travelling up and down. Without any exaggeration, it will be the twentieth time this year. This first wife is the prize of the University of Cape Town post-graduate scholarships and piece jobs, like the Andrew Mellon sponsored leadership programs covering students from mainly two universities in the Western Cape, where I served as a student mentor for their winter intake. Even the primary renovations at my maternal home and partly the building of our matrimonial home benefited from these kind gestures.

So I fabricate stories about the complexity of the signing out process at Forest Hill residence where I have been living this year. I actually want to tell her that I do not want to come. Do I have a choice?

Going to my room, I realise that I first have to start dealing with my dirty clothes. I take them to the laundry room. I sit down and start scribbling in my diary: everything from the time I had been sitting on Jameson steps hungrily gazing over the Cape Dutch world – just the Cape Dutch world – to the present moment. The washing machine wobbles and grumbles. I am seated next to a lady who is reading a book entitled *Friendship With God*. I have always been a friend of God, have I not? Another student complains about being dissatisfied with the courses she is presently studying: politics and sociology. I later learn that (according to her) she has been demoted by the university, from a Bachelor of Science degree in Civil Engineering to a degree in political science. A long time after finishing the laundry, I am sitting opposite the Forest Hill swimming pool, with my eyes glued on the rock-solid mountains just above me:

Layers of mist-clouds falling
Cascading
*   from Devil's Peak*
Golden grass shaved
Hand-brushed
*   by the shimmering south-easter.*

Pine trees holding a summit
I pine, I pine
*   for primordial cultures*
*   of the blue*
springbok and the eland.

Every man stands alone
*   next to him is the whirlwind.*

Lady in red clutches scissors
Shouting for James
*   a flatmate*
Basket ball players running
Black boys with bold heads skittering

                                        bouncing a
ball.

Up the rocky halls
Killian fire still falling
                        flowing against zig-zagged
mountain-tides
Mountain light absorbing
Relinquished
                through the rushing stellar spaces

frozen, on stoic mountain heights.

Artwork against the entrance
Horses pulling a cart
                        Cape Dutch windmill
overlooking

the red silhouettes.

Black slaves
From East Africa, the Caribbean
                                and the Cape
Labouring
                in the imperceptible farmland.

History is bound
By the indelible footsteps
                        of our predecessors

I had phoned T. two hours ago asking him to come and take me to the bus station in town. He usually does that. When I come from home, he takes me from the station to my flat, and vice versa. I also wanted to ask him if he would keep my belongings for the time I will be away. I could keep them in the university storeroom but my arrivals and departures are always very awkward for such an arrangement to be effective. I am hoping to come back within two weeks, just in time for vacation accommodation in Clarendon. I feel so bad when I have to phone T. I always make him share my burdens, which is not fair, I think. Every man has got trials enough for himself. He comes and takes me to the station anyway. The self-appointed porter pretends to help me take my bags to the office. I decline this gesture as I do not have money to pay him – which he will demand anyway. Just after I settle inside the office, my cell phone disrupts me. It's T. He has discovered that I have forgotten my suit cover and jacket in his car. I assure him that I left them on purpose. He really cares.

Inside the Greyhound bus I wait for the 'administration procedures' to take their toll. I am early today. As a matter of fact, I usually benefit from these procedures as I frequently catch the bus just before it leaves. I look across towards Table Mountain again. Mountains are so meaningful to me these days. Is it all about the new or post-romantic writers who are really managing to find a sense of being in these mountains, creating a God after Nietzsche pronounced Him dead? For the first time, I notice the OK/Shoprite tower. I had thought that OK Bazaars was long dead – at least that is the impression I got from my home town. These clouds or "killian fire" that have just been captured in a short piece of a poem recorded here are still hovering; the concrete tower appears taller than they are. I never realized that their altitude is so low, which could be an explanation of my long-time mystery: why is there always a mist over Devil's Peak?

V

On arrival in King William's Town, the bus stops at the Engen Garage. My wife is already waiting. After formal greetings, we take my belongings to catch a bus to the village. As I walk through the dark side of King William's Town, the religious songs that are integral to the landscape, and that have always crept into me like many infections, get into me once more. Though I have always tried to be stoical, their almost mystical power always overwhelms me. And here I am, forced to confront the extreme forms of poverty (the physical and the visible being just one of them) that these peripheries always have such power to display. The black nation will always be a religious nation. Their religion was never limited by indoor facilities – big stones, marble walls and thick windows. They have always practiced their art in the open space, in the sugar plantations while carrying out their masters' labour, during liberation rallies, before and after *every* kind of gathering. Although in one way these many struggles have come to a halt, the religion has never ended.

VI

King William's town of course could never be a 'homeland' to me, as Ithaca was or is to Odysseus. It belongs to the history of English plundering colonialism and black African *embourgeoisment*. To both these worlds and cultures I have been and I am still an outsider. As history reveals, the town itself was named after a reigning English monarch, William IV, in May 1835. It subsequently became military headquarters of the Queen Adelaide Province. In 1847 it was declared capital of British Kaffraria, an English colony. In 1970 it was made of the Department of Bantu Administration for the former homeland of Ciskei, a predecessor of the present-day Bhisho Administration.

The establishment of the town meant displacement (by force) of the earliest aboriginal inhabitants of the Ciskei area: the Bushmen, the Hottentots, and later the amaXhosa. Its rejection by local people was evident in the fact that during frontier wars the Buffalo Mission Station, an earlier form of King William's Town, was destroyed by fire twice. Its status as capital of British Kaffraria that it achieved in 1847 marked the triumph of the British colonial agenda over the amaXhosa. The fact that between 1850 and 1853 military pensioners were encouraged to settle in the town emphasizes its status as a military town.

The Nongqqawuse cattle killing (1856 – 1857) manifested itself as an outcry within the confines of this onslaught. From King William's Town the conquering onslaught continued: the colonisation of the Drakenstein Mountain, the Gamtoos, the Great Fish, the Keiskamma and the Great Kei Rivers. Eager even to conquer the Bashee River. So was Grahamstown when amaXhosa were driven from the Zuurveld.

The question, why do I have to subject the reader to this load of information when I arrive in King William's Town? Not matter what reservations I could have, this is my 'home'. As a black African writer, I am charged with the task of coming up with my own interpretation of these accounts. But, these are above all the dry bones of history that will nevertheless always from the nucleus or essence of my aesthetic. As a redeeming factor against being imprisoned by history, vision plays an invaluable role. That is up to an individual author to decide what 'vision' to adopt that will make him or her realise that as much as he/she interpreting history, he/she is still part of history making.

VII

The new release by Ringo, "Jerusalem", that I heard while in town just a few minutes ago still sounds divine to my ears. From the open door of my village house I can see the green fields just a glimpse away. The corn and potato shoots are just lifting themselves out of the murky ground. It is quite obvious that many villagers, owing to the present government's belief in the 'lucrative' power of agriculture, have cultivated their fields. On the surface, this looks like a great success story. Yet, what strikes me still is the old question of power. Linked to this is the grand fault of the perpetual infantilization of the village, even by contemporary African leaders themselves. When one hears many concerned people referring to the affairs of the village, it seems as if the village people are all uneducated, as if they can't think (yes, the political 'champions' think on their behalf), as if they have never been actively involved in providing practical solutions to their own problems. Most of all, as if these village people are incapable of any sinister or hidden agendas. The traditional – or let us say now casual hierarchy of the village – is a reality. There are still lords and serfs who will always divert any aid for their own selfish benefits.

In my village, the issue of land has become a means to power, but in a very negative sense. People cultivate the land not in the original and traditional understanding of supporting their own families, but as a territory of socio-political warfare. Take for example a case in my village that my wife has been relating to somebody else in my presence. Mr X "arrests" Mr Y's cattle. Mr X and Mr Y are in different political camps. The most interesting point is that these camps are splinter groups of one mother party, which also happens to be the ruling party. After barely a day, Mr Y takes Mr X's cattles to a privately - owned transit for cattle auctioning. The business owner (for the latter runs strictly like a business) charges Mr X R900 for about four cattle. Mind you, there are no monetary benefits that Mr Y is going to get, not even a commission. Perhaps the feeling of temporary triumph in the sight of his long-term political enemy is worth more than the money which Mr Y himself desperately needs.

Let us take another case in this setting. The local bourgeoisie have cultivated the land, a quite strategic response to the annual seasons as to keep their businesses alive and booming. What is ridiculous if that as much as they are anxious to rip off the villagers for the sake of business, they are not prepared to erect good fencing around their fields. They rely on the worn-out fencing that was perhaps erected by the government in the early 80's. What they will not hesitate to do is to charge ridiculously high fees for any 'damage' caused by anyone's livestock; most of which is merely incidental.

These two examples illustrate the scourge I have pointed out already; a romantic belief in the power of the land and the livestock to redeem the 'poor' people of the village. The reality is that the only people who can farm (either by cultivating land or keeping livestock) are commercial farmers. The examples of Mr X and the unnamed villagers mentioned above means that it is quite expensive for them to maintain livestock in their kraals – which is what I think is meant by indigenous methods of farming. Whether we like it or not, the golden age is long gone. Whatever is projected to be there only serves as a veneer for political squandering. This is quite a harsh judgement though, of which I am fully aware.

Out for a walk. It is this beauty that has always given me access to some means of self-knowledge long before the advent of books in my life. Looking after goats, horses and cattle in Hlathikhulu and Gotyibeni, cutting and dragging branches to build and mend African kraals, setting up bird traps and earnestly engaging in projects to find bird nests, hunting for hares and bucks, climbing tall trees for wild fruits and also cultivating the land. These many adventures, as grand they were, are now part of that past to which it is impossible to return. The act which can only be labelled as "childish" or "romantic"; but this is a formative world of human experience. And, like all formative encounters it remains a part of you. Nobody, to my account, expresses this nostalgia and consequently dilemma better than the late South African English poet Stephen Watson does in his *Writer's Diary*:

Keep in mind, always, the motivation that prompted you to write: those climbs, often before dawn, with your father when you were still a boy. For instance, coming out of the cloud ceiling into the summit of Devil's Peak, there to see that ceiling of cumulus below us, white in the early morning sun, and filling up the 30 – mile trough between the Table Mountain massif and Hottentots Holland. In other words, **it was beauty (even if a child's perception of it) that first led you to word** (emphasis mine). Later, there were other things, scarcely beautiful at all. But it began; you might say, in beauty. And therefore it will be, as the Navajo say, "finished in beauty"[3]

I can identify with these sentiments. It was this child's world that kept company with me when all that I had held dear, even my Christianity, seemed very distant. The beauty of a rural homeland is in danger of being lost to the city's glamorous 'stability'. The promise of an European education and the redemption promised by the Bible laid its claims on me during very disastrous and monstrous experiences. Mine is always a skewed landscape; I still suffer from my rebellions and am still a victim to innumerable tensions – tensions that can never easily translate themselves into words when one is charged with such a task. It is quite funny

---

[3] Watson, S. 1997. A Writer's Diary. Quillerie Publishers: Cape Town.

though; after a desperate effort to retrieve (both in imaginary and pragmatic terms) this lost world, my education and religion tightened their grip on me in ways like never before. The beauty of the concept of the great Trinity, I think.

I would like to conclude this essay with some extracts from my diary that have accumulated by the end of the week:

(a)

We attend a meeting in Alice with my wife, responding to the "prospects" of employment by Adult Basic Education; the very meeting that has brought me here. I am not surprised, it is just another political ploy. Nobody mentions anything what brought us there is the first place. Playing on our emotions for their political ends; quite a cheap propaganda, I think. What I saw there still remains with me; semi-teachers who are keen to pretend they are teachers, in the sense that being part of the public funded ABET demanded or afforded a specific definition of circumstances, by the authorities still.

(b)

At home, there is an *imbeleko* for a four year old girl. As far as I would still wish otherwise, my family still ensures its existence on traditions and ancestral worship. This is the very same thing that in the past decade I have always denied, at least for myself. Yet now, I do have an audacity to go inside the kraal, something I would not do a few years back.

I have even allowed my wife to help prepare for the function: a gesture which would label one as belonging to the camp. Let no one wish to misunderstand me though, even today, after all the difficulties and the tensions I have gone through, I still feel I want to be withdrawn into my old cocoon. It is a hard choice though, I realize. After the arrival of a wife and child, who rightly may wish to assert their individualities – the same thing myself I have done – it may never be an easy job to keep the family intact. My wife is always both sympathetic and empathetic to my dangerous adventures.

(c)

From a village funeral. As gathered from the series of sermons I have been listening to as from Monday, there is a deliberate effort or denial of the reality of God possibly married to pain and evil. I detect an error; a wishful thought that God is incapable of administering or commissioning any form of evil.

I think the Hebrew Biblical account of Job proves any sympathetic defender of an always merciful God wrong. His very nature and form rejoices in mercy, that is the very paradox. What seems to be difficult for us as mortals to fully comprehend and acknowledge is that the Hebrew God operates well through what I would temporarily like to call a split personality.

The story of redemption itself demanded that there should be a fall first and foremost. God masterminded this fall, and man fell victim. After all this denial of God's greatest virtues, we are left with nothing in our sermons but motivational speeches to sustain us until the next funeral. Our sermons, in their inherent pillistinism though, still lack the element of the mysterious metaphysical, which keeps any philosophy purporting a godhead over humankind intact.

What am I doing in this funeral anyway? Coming to fetch the pain that the bereaved may not be consumed. Last week there was a funeral. Next week there is another funeral. Even today, at the other side of the village there is another funeral. Mostly young people who die in the big cities like Cape Town, and come here only for burial. Allow me to say, there is judgement in the village.

(d)

Still [in our parents'] many failures or let us say inabilities, they condemn us. They are never complacent about their own beliefs; even though the forces of change have been unkind to them. Even at the face of the unbelieving youth, with our wavering faith in a colonial God, whose worship must always be backed up by material gain, their aboriginal faith still stands out. Yet, as remnants of a society whose authority was a king and a chief, a society where everybody worked hard to ensure sustainability; they still want to believe that *that* social order is still much alive. And, it is long dead.

THE CONDUCIVE ENVIRONMENT: J.J.R. JOLOBE'S INNOVATIVE WORK

INTRODUCTION:

I t is a well-known fact that colonialism in the then Cape Province had devastating effects not only in the lives of the inhabitants but also in their socioeconomic welfare. Between the 1806 British imperialism's annexure of the amaXhosa territory to the extension of colonial boundaries in 1850, a quite significant move had been taken to entrench the settler movement within the amaXhosa self-sustaining agrarian economy. The nine frontier wars (1779 - 1879) incrementally handed the mainly amaXhosa people and their indigenous economy into the hands of the British colonisers. The nail in the coffin was the massive slaughtering of livestock and burning of ripe crop (1856-1857) due to Nongqawuse's 'prophecy', the aftermath of which was the propelling of about 30 000 people to abandon their homes in search for employment. This was indeed the outcome of a much calculated move by Sir George Grey – the flamboyant Cape administrator - when through multi-pronged policies he sought to incapacitate the amaXhosa as far as self-sustenance was concerned. As much as the above-mentioned scenario was a defining factor, in this present paper it is my argument that British colonialism ushered in a new environment through which a certain segment of the amaXhosa people would prosper both spiritually and intellectually.

By stating this, it is not my intention to ignore Sir George Grey's convictions and thus ulterior motives when he introduced the 'civilising' policy for the natives (Ndletyana, 2008). As stated by the above-mentioned scholar, "Christianised and civilised, Grey believed, the Xhosa would cease being a British foe, and become a friend" (Ndletyana, 2008:4). However, as much as Sir George Grey and consequent administrators desired to infiltrate the colony, the missionary education and various institutions (mainly Lovedale college, missionary schools and various printing presses) left a lasting legacy in terms of education, religion and creative writing. Informing the crux of my main argument in this paper, Ndletyana (2008:4) observes,

"Beneficiaries of the civilising mission they were, yet they refused to define themselves in the image of their colonial benefactors. Rather, they re-defined themselves, combining the best of the two worlds into what became a modern African identity and a unique contribution to South African modernity".

J.J.R. Jolobe, one of the torch bearers[4] of that era is a subject of the present paper. Through his work, he worked aggressively in innovating with form. This resulted in him bordering in new angles as not only as a creative writer but also as a theologian, historian and linguist. The moving

---

[4] He combined all three aspects of missionary education: religious, educational and literary.

around of his family as a result of his father serving in the Presbyterian Church of Scotland as a minister exposed him to different languages. His distinct knowledge of isiXhosa dialects (Bhaca and Hlubi) spoken at that time as well as Sotho, gave him a much needed advantage to break new grounds linguistically.

As raised by different sources, he was a unique personality as he was not only caught up with nostalgia for the amaXhosa past but also negotiated with the acceptance of the Christian present. He campaigned for the combination of traditional and Christian life which he strongly believed would lead not only to survival but prosperity in many forms. Within the isiXhosa writing canon, the theme of the conflict of tradition and the West was explored as from 1940[5] to 1972[6]. What puts Jolobe's work in the category of its own is that the theme of his literary works is not only concerned with the inherent conflicts with African traditions and the West. As much as he strongly spoke out against the oppressive colonial system of the time, he openly encouraged his people to embrace "Western civilisation".

---

[5] A.C. Jordan's Inqqumbo Yeminyanya (later translated to The Wrath Of The Ancestors).
[6] Z.S. Qangule's Izagweba

FROM COLONIALISM TO APARTHEID: A BRIEF HISTORY OF THE AMAXHOSA OF THE EASTERN CAPE PROVINCE OF SOUTH AFRICA

Mlisa (2009) divides the history of the Eastern Cape into three major periods: the pre-colonial era (before the 17th century); the colonial era (the 17th to the 20th century) and the apartheid era (the 20th century). She further argues, "[the pre-colonial era] focus was on the Southern Nguni style of life before encountering the influence of the Eurocentric lifestyle" (Mlisa, 2009, p. 37). As Peires (1976) reveals, even prior to the arrival of missionaries, the amaXhosa cosmology was not necessarily pure. The interaction with both Khoi and San people meant hybridisation of some sort. To this effect, the influence of both Khoi and San religion prior to Christianity must be acknowledged (Peires, 1976).

Bundy (2004, p.10) has the following to say about the pre-colonial era:

This physical divide had profound implications for the human geography and history of the region. Hunters and herders - Bushman (sic) and Khoi - had long traversed the more arid territory of the Karoo and southwestern coastal reaches; and from the fourteenth and fifteenth centuries, Xhosa clans had begun to test the westerly limits of the 500 mm annual rainfall zone, running their herds, sowing their crops, establishing larger scale polities and denser settlement. Hunters, herders and mixed farmers traded, fought, and inter-married. The extent of their interaction can be traced in linguistic borrowings and in the genetic make-up and pigmentation of some Xhosa (sic) clans.

The arrival the Dutch settlers in the Cape on the 6th of April 1652 would not only serve as a pioneering initiative for the establishment of a refreshment station for the Dutch ships *enroute* to the East but would also initiate a centuries long adventure in usurping both livestock and land of the original inhabitants of the land, both the Khoi-San and the amaXhosa. Following the frontier wars stretching between 1779 and 1880, the colonial period in the Eastern Cape Province of South Africa was entrenched by the 1820 settling of Europeans originally from England, Scotland and Ireland. Bundy (2004, p.10) summarises the progression of the colonial project in the Eastern Cape as follows:

> Subsequently, these patterns of contact were disrupted and overlaid by others: by the pressures of trekboers in the eighteenth century on Khoisan peoples and then by competition over water, grazing land and cattle between boer and Xhosa. Finally, of course, British settlers and troops unleashed forces - cultural, economic and military - that shattered Xhosa society west and immediately east of the Kei river.

The 1778 agreement between Governor Van Pletternburg and two minor amaXhosa chiefs would affect the amaXhosa people living west of the Fish River in many ways. Prior to that, there had been peaceful co-existence with the Boers, who had enslaved the Khoi people in previous encounters. The first British occupation from 1795 to 1803 and that of the Batavian Republic between 1803 and 1806 was a sign of terror. All of the above attempted to propel the Xhosa people towards the East of the Fish River.

Peires (1988, p. 161) adding to the above sentiments reveals, "in the shade of the house of Phalo, every man had a ridge for his homestead and a stream for his cattle. When his sons left home after circumcision, they never feared that they will fail to find land and water of their own". He continues, "By 1847 things were very different. The Xhosa kingdom had shrunk, and in shrinking it had lost vast tracts of its most fertile territory. The Xhosa were driven across the Fish in 1812, out of the Kat River Valley in 1829, and right past the Keiskamma in 1847" (Peires, 1988, p. 162). The indigenous economy that this community utilised as means of livelihood was negatively affected by the arrival of industrialisation and large-scale migrant labour.

The rise of two main personalities in the 19th century, Nxele (Makhanda) and Ntsikana, within the amaXhosa socio-political landscape had an effect on both Xhosa religion and way of life. As stated by Peires (1979, p. 51):

The hundred years war (1779-1880) of the Xhosa people against the white colonists of the Cape of Good Hope produced not one but two historical traditions. One, originating with Nxele, was war-like and nationalist, embodying African beliefs and African culture. The other, originating with Ntsikana, was pacifist and Christian, enjoining salvation through obedience to the will of God.

As a result of being displaced by the English from Zuurveld (the present day Makhanda area and the surroundings) the amaXhosa experienced some kind of "national stress" (Peires, 1976). However, as argued by the above mentioned scholar, the interaction with the Boers was different. As stated by Peires (1976, p. 31), "mutual acculturation – many Boers even adopted Xhosa religious beliefs - reduced the difference between the two cultures".

As much as the amaXhosa were in awe in the presence of a European civilisation propagated by Christianity, they were not completely rendered helpless. To some extent, they did resist and thus were able to retain some of their indigenous institutions that pre-existed the late 19th century English missionaries. To this effect, Peires (1976, p. 145) observes,

Thus it was largely in vain that the missionaries, most of whom equated   Christianity with European civilisation and behaviour, attempted to persuade the Xhosa (sic) to abandon trusted practices which they regarded as essential to their earthly prosperity and well-being in favour of a doctrine which was abstract and explicitly devoid of material benefits.

To the Xhosa people, these cruel encounters with the British meant the invention of the word *imfazwe* (destruction of the soil as the British destroyed food, gardens and people). To a large extent, they also stole cattle. In response, the Xhosa and the Khoi formed a joint war. Peires (1979, p. 54) observes, "the expulsion created a set of problems which the chiefs were unable to solve. Thus, in the years immediately following 1812, political leadership was passed from the hands of chiefs into the hands of prophet-figures". As already alluded to, Nxele and Ntsikana, at approximately the same period of ten years served two different Xhosa chiefs in offering a spiritual dimension to the already threatened cosmology of war and daily existence.

After almost a century of wars in the Eastern frontier of the Cape Colony, "when the last frontier war – the War of Ngcayechibi – ended in 1879, the colonial forces shifted their focus to labour" (Ngcukaitobi, 2018, p. 19). As a result of the discovery of gold and diamond in the Free State and Kimberley, the Anglo-Boer war erupted. The English settlers felt they also had a stake in the minerals plundered by the Boers in these two areas. This infighting did not only claim many lives in both sides but left the economy in tatters. Thus, after the Anglo-Boer War it was mandatory to build a new country and a new economy.

As Ngcukaitobi, (2018, p. 25) keenly observes, "although Africans had been kept out of the political system, the mining bosses were actually aware that they had to be brought into the economy for the system to function". This period can be characterized by a number of events that would shape the future of the Union. These are the 1903 formation of the South African Native Affair Commission; the conversion of Africans into labour units in the colonial economy and a deliberate attempt to 'civilise' Africans. As observed by Khabela (1996) and Ngcukaitobi (2018), the civilization of Africans would be a smokescreen for ulterior motives such as creating labour reserves for the Cape Colony.

On the above sentiments Ngcukaitobi (2018, p. 27) declares, "having conquered by military means, the colonial state aimed not only to turn the black masses into a large pool of semi-skilled labourers, but also to create a docile educated class that would not question the economic and cultural hegemony of Empire". In the long run, this strategy would work against the state. Ngcukaitobi (2018, p. 28) declares, "but ten years after Britain's final military assaults of the late 1870's in Xhosaland and Zululand, a new form of resistance employing the institutions of colonialism emerged". The above-mentioned scholar continues, "not only did they use education as a basis of self-awareness and self-reliance, they saw it as a means of waging new struggles for emancipation." (Ngcukaitobi, 2018, p. 36).

The establishment of the Union in 1910 was a direct response to the imperial government to resolve the native question (Ngcukaitobi, 2018). The "Bantustan" system which was implemented after the 1948 apartheid election paved the way for new policies like separate development widely known as apartheid. The Bantu Authorities Act of

1951 offered a legal arm through which the Bantustan system could be established. In 1956, the former Transkei was the first 'homeland' to be created. This followed the 1913 and 1936 Land Acts, through which 87% of land was allocated to the white minority. As stated by Bank and Southall, this was driven by a philosophy of "a multi-national state", ironically bearing resemblance to the post-apartheid so-called rainbow nation, which was based not on 'history' but 'past conquest' (Bank & Southall, 1996, p. 412)

The apartheid era, a policy or system of segregation or discrimination on grounds of race, was defined not only by removals from ancestorial areas but urban infrastructural planning which by nature was destructive to the "kinsmen" or "tribesmen" lifestyle that the individuals were categorised as such to (Bank, 2001). The impact of social engineering policies in some of the newly established townships, both in the custody of the Republic and the apartheid homeland (areas that were preserved as reserves for most African people during the apartheid era), created "apartheid subjects" from the amaXhosa people in the Eastern Cape.

Through the Native Affairs Act of 1909 and the Native Land Act of 1913, "a system of direct rule was imposed upon the formerly autonomous chiefdoms, the legitimacy of chiefs was deliberately undermined, and subaltern authority was widely – but not uniformly – developed upon headmen" (Bank & Southall, 1996, p. 410). Furthermore, through the Native Administration Act of 1927, "systematic powers to appoint, recognize and remove chiefs" was solely vested on the Governor-General of the Cape Province (Bank & Southall, 1996, p. 411). The arrangement was designed in such a way as "to compel their services as administrative functionaries" (Bank & Southall, 1996, p. 411).

This all formed a foundation to the effect of reinventing of the former Bantustan areas rural government. The Freedom Charter, a document which culminated from the 1923 Bill of Rights of South Africa, was adopted in 1955 (Ngcukaitobi, 2018). It is Ngcukaitobi's contention that the development of the two above documents, that he terms as the African's Claim Document, was a statement against five decades of attempts of colonial administration (Ngcukaitobi, 2018).

The crafting of the constitution, a document which was a culmination of difficult negotiations spanning the periods 1990-1994, allowed for re-integration of the ten former 'homelands'. For both administrative and political purposes, these were further delineated into new nine new regions or provinces. The notions of liberal and consociational democracy were originally intended to be major tenants of the constitution. Also, existent legally constituted traditional authorities are 'recognized' and the indigenous laws and customs are supervised. However, "… some question whether the constitutional framework was in fact the correct response to colonialism and apartheid" (Ngcukaitobi, 2018, p. 1).

As observed by the above mentioned scholar, racial segregation can be traced back to the late-nineteenth-and early-twentieth century. As such, Victorian politicians offered a blue print. The former Transkei had already been a piloting ground for the implementation of the above within which the English colonial system had been enacted as early as 1894 (Bank & Southall, 1996; Ngcukaitobi, 2018).

Although there was more influence of Western culture in the former Transkei and Ciskei than anywhere in South Africa through mission-funded education, the ulterior motive was the transformation of the African peoples of South Africa from self-sufficient and autonomous through political subordination. Consequently, they were turned "into either communities of peasants, living on attenuated tribal lands which became increasingly dependent upon the export of migrant labour, or wage labourers who worked for firms and farms and lived in areas owned by whites" (Bank & Southall, 1996, p. 411).

The above mentioned situation was culminated in the chiefs' relative control of land through the Union 'Native policy' which allowed them to collect taxes partially for their financial gain, especially in Pondoland where colonial administration was enacted as early as the 19th century. At least, the policy of communal land tenure left the inhabitants of the late 19th century and 20th century 'homelands' better off as compared to those trapped in "the landless condition of the African population of the white areas of South Africa" (Bank & Southall, 1996, p. 412). The chiefs were not only stripped of the authority over their ancestral land but also in presiding over legal matters within their respective constituencies. Through a colonial system designed

Customary Law, they were only granted powers to arbitrate only in civil cases and not criminal ones.

Through being *ex officio* members of "local governments within whose jurisdiction they fall", traditional authorities can conversely be used as state apparatus for both direct and indirect rule (Bank & Southall, 1996, p. 409). Historically, the recognition of traditional authorities in South Africa never came by default but was due "to a threatened boycott of the first democratic elections by the Zulu based Inkatha Freedom Party" (Bank & Southall, 1996, p. 409). This further emphasizes the concept of ambiguity as far as the roles of chiefs in local, provincial or national governance is concerned.

With more power progressively vested on them, the 1963 Transkei homeland first election directly translated into an outnumbering of the new 45 member legislative Assembly by 64 *ex-officio* chiefs (Bank & Southall, 1996). Presentation of the overall symbolism of post-apartheid South Africa (flags, bureaucracies and armies) by separate development architects was argued as "providing for a synthesis between tradition and modernity" (Bank & Southall, 1996, p. 413).

Not all chiefs necessarily allowed the scenario of being used as apartheid state apparatus within their respective "reserves". Some chiefs were part of the 1912 African National Congress (ANC) founding meeting. Also, Chief Poto of Western Pondoland who in 1963 opposed the imposition of separate development upon that territory in the Transkei's first election is another example (Bank &

Southall, 1996). King Sabata Dalindyebo from the former Transkei took the baton and consequently was exiled in Zambia. The resistance of chiefs to both colonial and apartheid oppression was enacted in the coronation of Chief Albert Luthuli as the African National Congress (ANC) president in 1952. Lastly, Nelson Mandela, the first president of a democratic South Africa, himself was a son of a chief deposed by a colonial magistrate. With time, through the machinery of the Congress of Traditional Leaders of South Africa (CONTRALESA) traditional leadership was also coerced by the ANC to serve its political purposes just before the first democratic elections were held in April 1994.

The role of the chiefs was also very crucial in forging socio-political relations in the former "homelands" of Transkei and Ciskei just after the apartheid government installed Chief Ministers were overthrown through military coups. In the former Ciskei where Gqozo had taken over from Dr Lennox Sebe, there were conflicts between traditional leaders and civic organizations. Contrary to Gqozo, Holomisa never removed chiefs from their positions but rather removed political enemies (Bank & Southall, 1996, p. 423).

The apartheid era is defined by not only removals but urban infrastructural planning which by nature is destructive to the lifestyle that the individuals are used to (Bank, 2001). The impact of social engineering policies in some of the newly established townships, both in the custody of the Republic and the apartheid homeland, sought to create "apartheid subjects" from the amaXhosa people in the Eastern Cape.

According to Bank (2001), the amaXhosa people who were subjected to such in the East London area lost touch with some of their traditions and the essence of who they were. The housing system was further used as a tool for control, argues Bank.

According to the above-mentioned scholar, if individuals did not qualify for housing, they were not kicked out of the system but instead were further referred for counselling (Bank, 2001). This clinical treatment of a social ailment enforced the subjectivity agenda in terms of Bantu administrators who in turn were acting for the apartheid state (Bank, 2001). This was also used to depoliticise the black masses. Creation of violence, gangsterism and unemployment was also a defining factor (Bank, 2001).

J.J.R. JOLOBE'S MISSIONARY BACKGROUND AND OUVRE:

As stated by Attwell (1999:268), "in what has been called the `comedic' vision of missionary education, post-Darwinian notions of progress and Christian eschatology were easily combined". As implicated, the main question "is whether the intellectuals of Dube's class, the *kholwa*, converted and merely accepted the metaphorics of the civilising mission or whether they appropriated them to serve their own interests" (ibid). The above- mentioned scholar further insinuates, "In all probability, the answer cannot be either-or: as products of the mission system they had been interpellated by its language, values and ethos, but at the receiving end of colonial racism and the limitations it imposed on their social, political and economic ambitions, they were aggrieved by the contradictions between their ideals and actual experience" (Attwell, 1999:268).

The Glasgow Mission Society's Reverand John Bennie's inscription, deliberately superimposed over "a stoic looking cow", Christian or secular, appropriated not only the amaXhosa cosmos but both their land and livestock (Peires, 1980). In essence, by declaring that "All cattle come from God", on behalf of the settlers, he was offering both justification and propaganda as a vehicle for both usurping and appropriation of the fore mentioned 'indigenous' property. By default, if the statement was indeed true, as he claimed, as agents of the British Empire and thus God they had a stake in both the Khoi-San and amaXhosa livestock. Between 1823 and 1915, focal institutions like Chuma mission station (that later changed to Lovedale) and the South African Native College (now Fort Hare) were formed. The two above mentioned institutions would play a significant role in not only reducing the South African indigenous languages to a quasi-status of written text but would help to 'civilise' a large number of African middle class.

James Ranisi Jolobe was born on the 25th of July 1902 at Indwe, roughly 67 years after the famous 14th May 1835 milkwood covenant. Led by John Ayliff from Butterworth to

Peddie, the 'Mfengu'[7] tribe gathered and convened under a milkwood tree. They made a covenant to serve not only God but the Empire. They also made a solemn promise to educate their children. Jolobe was born to amaHlubi, one of the sub-groups that belong to the 'Mfengu' tribe. I am raising this now for two major reasons. Firstly, in terms of the socio-economic vantage and the aesthetic this background would assist the young Jolobe. His father (a minister in Presbyterian Church of Scottland) and mother (a primary school teacher) would instil a love for both God and education to the young Jolobe, just as promised by his ancestors. Secondly, this would haunt his career later in his life at Lovedale as there was a tribal feud then between the former and the 'Xhosas'. This feud was so immense as it would even affect giants like D.D.T. Jabavu, as he himself was classified as a 'Mfengu'.

After qualifying and practising as both a teacher and a minister, he would eventually graduate with a B.A. degree (Ethics and English) from the University of Fort Hare in

---

[7] 'Mfengu' is a generic term for the broken peoples who among the Xhosa in the wake of the Mfecane. They rallied around the sympathetic Wesleyan missionary John Ayliff, and during the Sixth Frontier War (1834-5) h instrumental in provoking them to desert across the Kei to the British.

1932. Married to a professional nurse, they had three children. His classic novel, *Elundini Lothukela*, was published in 1959. At a certain point in his career he was invited to be a tutor at Lovedale by Reverand Grant. It may be around this time that the tension was heating up between 'Mfengus' and 'Xhosas' as Peirres records that at a certain point Lovedale authorities were much concerned about this rivalry as somehow "it would affect the church" (Peirres, 1980). Nkosi (1981, unpaginated) observes. "By the 1920s in South Africa the Scottish missionaries had firmly laid the groundwork for the literary activity which would culminate in that first flowering of African literature the most notable representatives of which were Mqhayi, Jolobe, Bereng, Vilakazi and H. I. E. Dhlomo. . . ." (Lewis Nkosi, 1981).

His parallel use of three languages (Bhaca, Hlubi and Sotho) initially posed a linguistic challenge as far as his literary outputs in isiXhosa were concerned. However, with the intervention of luminaries like S.E.K. Mqhayi, this would later prove to be a major development in the language. He also crossed boundaries as far as cultures and customs of these three main Xhosa sub-groups are concerned. This would later be an asset in his writing career as his major classic, *Elundini Lothukela* , owed its conception to such ethnographic inclinations. He wrote across all forms: that is journalism, novel, drama, poetry and essays. To prove this, in 1952 he was even awarded the Vilakazi Memorial Prize for both preserving and developing Nguni languages.

As far as language is concerned, Jolobe proved himself to be a social developer. His whole oeuvre includes the following: two novels; four collections of poetry and eight translations. In total, he received five literary awards for different forms of writing. The colonial benefactors like Jolobe were not simple dormant recipients of the foreign 'civilisation' agenda brought by missionaries. As argued by Ndletyana (2008:5) "[they] re-defined themselves, combining the best of the two worlds into what became a modern African identity and a unique contribution to South African modernity".

As much as his primary language of writing is isiXhosa, he adopted bilingualism through translating both from isiXhosa to English and vice versa. Most of the work that he translated from English to isiXhosa were missionary documents and pamphlets published by Lovedale. To the same extent, he translated educational material aimed for schools. He also translated works of significance like Rider Haggards's 1885 *King Solomon's Mines* to *Imigodi ka Kumkani uSolomoni, Up from Slavery* by B.T. Washington as *Ukuphuma ukusuka ebukhobokeni* (1951). In 1972 he translated the Preface of John Knox Bokwe's Biography written by S.E.K. Mqhayi. In his own work, he translated his classic epic poem, "uThuthula" from isiXhosa to English. There is also a slim collection of his work originally translated by Z.S. Qangule and Robert Mshengu Kavanagh in 1971, *The Making Of A Servant And Other Poems*.

In seeking larger audiences, Jolobe translated some of his work, especially the award winning epic poem, *uThuthula*. *Thuthula* is still a subject interest judging from the 2003 Chris "Zithulele" Mann's adaptation of the epic into a play *Thuthula: Heart Of The Labyrinth* and its reception by the amaXhosa royal house. Xhegwana (2022) has also revisited the debate through publishing *A Letter To Thuthula* in the Institute for the Study of English in Africa published poetry journal, the *New Coin*. As a decolonising tool, Jolobe also translated a large corpus of work by other authors from English to isiXhosa. To this effect, Kwetana observes,

In his writings, Jolobe always tried to make readers aware of the statements and sentiments made by Europeans about Nguni African people [that] were derogatory in nature. Attitudes of Europeans towards African people were well captured in King Solomon's Mines (para 1.4.3, v). His translations thus ensured that those who were reading said work were aware of how Europeans were viewing them and how they regarded their status in society. At this time, he was engaging in the political awakening of African people (Kwetana 2000).

CONCLUSION:

The first generation of Xhosa intellectuals were a rare breed. With such a skill they negotiated the binary nature of their existence; old and new, traditional and modern, African and European. In being benefactors of the British missionary education, they were not passive recipients but somehow displayed a certain kind of resistance which was not easily detectable to the Empire. In doing so, they left a blue-print through which generations to come would develop. Although very much younger than these pioneers[8], Jolobe was put in the same category as the likes of Mqhayi, Jabavu and Bhokhwe. As already inclined to in the above argument, he adopted an aesthetic that had already defined itself in terms of mission education and the 'civilising' mission of the colonisers. This can be attributed both to the vintage point that both his lineage, the so-called Mfengus, and his very immediate family offered him. Indeed, his was a conducive environment that, with a lot of hard work of course from his side, allowed both his spiritual and academic pursuits flourish.

---

[8] Perhaps one could rightly point him out a belonging more to the second generation.

WHEN THE RAIN COMES DOWN

I t shall never be forgotten that during the so-called 1820-1835 Mfecane wars over greener pastures and much flowing rivers and consequently consolidation of nation-hoods, a number of families and clans were scattered and lost in the belt of the Southern African landscape. This African diaspora, the most vulnerable being women and children, presently cannot trace their lineage. Though there were many other intrinsic forces to this massive exodus, rumours about incursions of Northern African Arabic slavery drive added to the impetus. Yes, attributed to these wars, there are still unclaimed thrones with illegitimate 'heirs' sitting on them.

The driving of the Zelemu and Wushe of ancient Debe, presently known as the 'Bhaca', through the biggest river in present day Kwazulu-Natal, Tugela River, was never less than a bloody affair. The sojourn through the dense and dark Nkandla forests; with intense fear of the looming common enemy overcoming any possible feelings of nostalgia for what they could commonly refer to as 'home'. It is during these dark times that the name 'Bhaca' appeared, denoting the one who is in constant run and thus hiding from the enemy. In deep concern of their livestock, they followed the bellies of the cascading rivers; some of which are the Sterkspruit and Umlazi rivers to the present day Shongweni Dam in Pinetown.

Their historical affinity with the Ngwane, presently known as Swati, places their placental roots above the banks of the Pongola River. In this ancestral land, they were also shaded by the rich Lembombo hills. Through this journey to the unknown, not even the most basic pleasure of lighting fire could be enjoyed as the enemy could easily track them in that single flicker of light. Hence, they resorted to eating the meat from the wild games they hunted and their own cattle raw, the practice they called *ukufukutsha.*

The journey to the realization of the dream to build a nation and finally the construction of the Embondzeni Great Place in Mount Frere was never an easy one. King Madzikane, in the early 19th century, never only fled the killing sword of the invisible enemy, but in his determination to build a strong nation crossed many rivers. Through sword, hunger and thirst this warrior-nation experienced many vicissitudes. Many clan members were lost. Also, along the way, allies and destitute nations were amalgamated and absorbed to form the great Bhaca nation. Intrinsically so, one of those are the historically superior Wushe who upon absorption automatically assumed the role of a genetic "inferior" nation.

The missionary trickery and consequently mirage towards the end of the 19th century would drive some minor clans of this nation, with the derogative term "Amamfengu" attached to them, beyond the Kei River. My maternal side of the family lineage, whose diminished descendants, after an almost century long odyssey over-ached by betrayal, treachery and martyrdom would rest on the banks of the Xesi, Mdizeni and

Nomvana Rivers triology. This was a good four hundred kilometres from Mount Frere where the warrior-king Madzikane had disposed their forebears from across the Tugela River. As traditional family compounds they occupied two villages quite far from each other by ancient standards (considering the fact that the only mode of transport accessible was the horse).

These are the two villages of Zihlahleni and Gobozana. By modern standards and political demarcation, they occupy two different local municipalities; the Raymond Mhlaba Local Municipality and the Ngqushwa Local Municipality. Although they use at least three different surnames, they share the same clan name: *OoKhowane.* Amongst these three surnames there is the one that was allocated to my mother by her mother when she was dispatched to the care of doctor-missionaries and educators at Mount Coke as a young disabled child, Xhegwana.

I hardly know about its origin and the reason why it was allocated to my mother. Whenever I would pose questions about this, I would be pointed to a spot next to the kraal where one of our great ancestors Xhegwana was buried. This is the surname that was passed on to all her offspring, including her grand-children. For example, at primary school I was using the surname Sogidashe. Hence it appears in certain important personal documents, like the Biblecor Bible Correspondence Courses Certificates presumably still housed at the once fire consumed University of Cape Town African Studies Manuscripts and Archives section. When I proceeded to the local Lukhozi High School, my uncle gently nudged me towards changing my surname from Sogidashe to Xhegwana. Surprisingly, this administrative procedure had no glitches then. It was a matter of a seamless meeting between my uncle and the principals of these two schools.

My birth, foregoing the patrilineal Nkabane clan who only surfaced very late in life, owes itself to this very traditional upbringing. I was born on 22nd of May 1972 to Nonceba Mercy Xegwana. By the time of my birth she was 31, and would turn 32 only two months later. For many years now she had been a domestic worker for various households of mostly German origin in King William's town. By the time of my birth, she had already lost both of her parents, Thandidebe "Willie" Sogidashe and Nofanele Magdalene Sogidashe. My grandmother's matrilineal surname is Gidi and she is of the Goqolo clan.

My father, Mbayiyana Welcome Cele, was also a gardener around King William's Town around the time he met my mother. He belongs to the Nkabane clan who by historical classification are pure amaXhosa, *abantwana bomgquba*. Through archival affirmation, they have a streak of royalty in their bloodline. There are many versions to the story of amaNkabane and their royalty, one of which takes them back to 18th - 19th century Southern African landscape, predominantly Natal. Within the affairs of amaXhosa, one authoritative source even states that they are one of the nations that, together with amaNgwevu, were stripped of their kingdom. Within this myriad of stories, there is also a piece of history, myth or legend which places their great matrilineal ancestor, Mfaz'obelenye (the one-breasted woman), at the centre of the amaXhosa royal tree.

By the time my parents met my father was married and had children already. Theirs was an occasional affair where I was conceived in the heat of the moment. He would only surface twenty-one years later after relatively little digging from my side. I would later learn that he had many children outside of his own marriage.

My mother raised me alone. Like Mirriam in the Biblical story of Moses, she had to devise many means to hide me from the surveilling eye of her white master in King William's town while she worked to support he traditional family back at home. At certain points, she had to hide me with relatives at Ginsberg location. Eventually I ended up in the care of her uncle in the village where she was born.

Though she was physically disabled, she never paraded that as an excuse not to be a responsible citizen. She had contracted polio at a very early age. As already alluded to, she ended up at Mount Coke Methodist Missionary Hospital, situated at about 18 kilometres from King William's town, where she spent most of her formative years as both a patient and student. At her weakest point, the condescending Christian subculture of Methodism was imposed on her. This would stick with her for the rest of her life. Under very difficult circumstances, she survived and also excelled academically. She was released back to her home after just acquiring her pre-Bantu Royal Education Standard Six certificate.

Above all, one must be reminded that I hold the dubious prestige of being the first member of my matriarchal line of family to hold a higher European education. Although my mother went up to the upper echelons of what was on offer then, she unfortunately could not amalgamate her achievements because of the simple refusal of her mother to do so.

Her elder brother, a mine worker then at the Goldfields Cementation Mining Company in Southdale (Johannesburg), had put aside money for her to be sent out to those Bantustan higher education or nursing colleges of the time. Instead, my grandmother used the money to build a house. Again, one of my grandmother's cousins offered to sponsor my mother's education in return that on her home-coming she should re-pay the loan in one way or another. Again, my most erstwhile grandmother refused such gestures! In much anger and defiance, my mother decided to join the village work force of domestic workers in King William's town where she faithfully served different masters until her retirement in 1984 after she gave birth to one of my sisters.

Out for a walk. It is this beauty that has always given me access to some means of self-knowledge long before the advent of books in my life. Looking after goats, horses and cattle in Hlathikhulu and Gotyibeni, cutting and dragging branches to build and mend African kraals, setting up bird traps and earnestly engaging in projects to find bird nests, hunting for hares and bucks, climbing tall trees for wild fruits and also cultivating the land, these bucolic activities formed me.

Yet these many adventures, as grand as they were, are now part of that past to which it is impossible to return in the completeness and innocence which first held me spellbound in a Wordsworthian sense. This formative early life of the veld remains a part of myself, the heartwood of my being, if you like. It has recently resurfaced in the form of visions and trances linking me to the long line of the ancient practice of Nguni magic weavers, or *amagqirha*.

After spending a year in a school bridging facility at Zihlahleni Location where I grew up, then called *ugqusha*, I registered to do Sub A in 1981 at Zihlahleni Primary School. I would graduate from the local primary school with flying colours. Throughout my time at that local primary school the only "opponent" I had was a girl whose grandmother was a teacher in the school. Most people believed this feat was organised as she used to cry if she came second. So it happened, for position one, we gave turns to each other from Standard 1 to Standard 5.

It is at this school that my journey with literature began, as an orator. As a young student in Standard 1, I would make big boys sit around me while I told them stories. The one they loved the most is the journey of uncle Jackal and uncle

Wolf to the home of uncle Jackal's in-laws. Along the way they see fruit trees and dear do they not help themselves! So the narrative goes and reaches a *culdesac* , "Bagquzula ke obhuti bakho bagquzula". The boys would have stomach cramps laughing as I have a speech impediment. I cannot pronounce the click words. They demanded I retell the myth, which I did not mind as they threw their lunch money in front of me.

It was at the beginning of 1987 when I would proceed to the local senior secondary school, Lukhozi. There I met scholars from close to ten feeding villages, each with its own primary school. Some feeding primary schools were even rooted at Dimbaza Township, which historically by mere apartheid architecture is a semi-urban area. This means that educationally they were inclined to have more resources.

Because of the South African political unrests that were the order of the day then, there were also scholars from as far as Port Elizabeth and Uitenhage – ideally other apartheid pockets of academic excellence. That motivated me to prove myself if really my past achievements were worth it. That worked as I had no opponent. The students ended up giving me several nicknames, amongst which were *Master* and *Sir Isaac Newton*, the latter not only emulating my English second name but spelling out the fact that I was a guru of Mathematics, Physical Sciences and Biology. During 1988 I sat down with my uncle and shared with him my dream to be a medical doctor. According to the research I had done, one needed mathematics and science subjects to be able to pursue medicine.

The only challenge we faced was that then Lukhozi did not offer such from Std 8. My uncle made a visit to the school principal of my former primary school, Mr Makhwabe, who was very helpful in getting a suitable school for me. After he did a lot of shopping around and applications, and of course using his clout as a not only a school principal but also as a sport legend, we settled with two schools, Thembalabantu, a quite famous boarding school in Zwelitsha those days, and Kama High School (to some extent, also a rural legendary school those days).

Because I faced difficulties with getting boarding facilities at Thembalabantu coupled with the fact that both Mr Makhwabe and my uncle thought the new 'hostile' environment Zwelitsha would display outside of the school's boarding facilities was quite treacherous, we opted for Kama High School. It is located at Middledrift about 19 kilo metres from my rural home. For a year I lived with a family at Sweet Home, a village across the Xesi River. I settled very well at school and still with many academic opponents from much different backgrounds I excelled academically.

I remember very well during the prize giving ceremony at the end of the academic year in 1989 where I almost collected prizes for every subject. That was quite an unusual feat and of course it attracted a lot of friends and onlookers. This school operated like an informal boarding school, with boarders clustering at the much historic Ann-Shaw rural establishment and the villages close by. Later, after I decided to move out of the home I lived in at Sweet Home, I was even a boarder in one of the one room flats at the Middledrift Railway Station.

Besides other extra-mural activities like being deeply involved in the Student Christian Movement, it was here that I started writing a lot. While I lived at Sweet Home, I wrote a twenty-five episode radio drama for a competition at the then Radio Xhosa, now Umhlobo Wenene. After sending my only copy of the hand written radio drama, I never heard from them again. Nevertheless, I never stopped writing and sending my hand written material out to prospective publishers. The era within which my initial work was written and published is that of pre-democracy. To be more specific, the work that has formed a foundation to my oeuvre was created during the South African state of emergency era between 1985 and 1990.

As I wrote mostly in English except for the radio play I had sent to Radio Xhosa and a collection of short stories or mini memoirs, *Ukuwa Nokuvuka kukaKama*, I was lambasted by prospective publishers for writing in English. At the other hand, I failed to understand why I should be forced to write in my mother tongue. To me, this linguistic limitation in forms of artistic expressions equalled some kind of oppression. As if apartheid was not enough, another level of oppression was imposed on artists who chose to express themselves in other art media other than those prescribed to them.

As I rebelled and continued to write in English, 'Lady Luck' would finally cross my path. I wrote desperate letters to as far as Cape Town. A lady by the name of Mrs June Savage, an editor at Maskew Miller Longman, responded to one of my letters. She did not only give me advice on how to keep the creative fire burning by being involved in writers' organisations like the Congress of South African Writers (COSAW), but also raised the importance of forming writers' groups. We would remain pen friends until I was admitted at the University of Cape Town. In one of her letters she inserted a pamphlet from a community based publisher based in Cape Town, Buchu Books. This is where I would have my breakthrough and feel the joy of holding my first baby in a book form.

After much deliberation, I decided to try my luck and write a fully-fledged novel for submission purposes at Buchu Books. I can still remember how every night after school, sitting on a school chair and using a school desk as a table, in my one room flat by the Middledrift train station, I would scribble on my very nice writing pad I had bought from CNA bookshop in King William's Town solely for that purpose.

Within a week, I had finished my 'novel', which later after publication would be categorised as a novella by literary critics and reviewers. One reviewer from Texas University gave me the honour of being the first South African to publish a book in English at the age of 19. I was very much ecstatic about my debut literary achievement as favourable reviews kept on pouring in.

Although it still confuses me, the book review I will never forget is the one by the late poet and political activist famous for the "Guava Juice" poem, Sandile Dikeni. He was not only reviewing the book but, like certain academics, also selling it to the country's educational system. He also did point out at some weaknesses in the conception of the book itself; especially the relationship between the protagonist Eric and his "never complaining" wife Cinderelle. In retrospect, this is reminiscent of the bigotry debates not only inherent within a young author not yet liberated from rural sexual discourses in South Africa but also a global phenomenon.

However, that also did not stop devious critics who did not see a reason why this hogwash and mediocre literary work could even see the light of the day. Yes, the publisher's open-door policy which emphasised on a non-editorial approach to publication of manuscripts rendered the book vulnerable immediately when it got out there. Honestly speaking, like one of the critics, it is difficult for me to read the book in its present form. Yet, literary, it will always be a great personal achievement as it allowed my name to infiltrate the global publishing industry. Within a decade it was held by almost every university library and community libraries not only in South Africa but globally.

These literary critics were very hard on the late teenager author hungry for recognition who was me. The Encyclopaedia of Post-Colonial Literatures in English reveals that *The Faint-Hearted Man* continues to attract considerable critical attention. Most recently, it has even survived the fire that consumed the University of Cape Town African Studies archives section.

The book caused a lot of stir after it was published not only in literary circles but at my local school and my village as well. I became an instant celebrity and consequently the pressures and pain that go with that were the order of the day. People would come to my village home to congratulate me, and some would under all kinds of pretext and disguises have the book in their hands for good. That is how I would lose most of my personal copies that the publisher had sent to me. There were also a lot of lie-peddlers who invented very funny stories about the events surrounding the publication of my book and presumably its adaptation into television series and prescription in schools right under my nose.

Everybody knew that there was no such, only that people are so much obsessed with poking their noses in other people's businesses. Even if it means inventing propaganda to achieve that they will exactly do that. Yes, to my late discovery, the book was circulated by the likes of Amazon and Chapter One Books throughout the world without me even knowing. That one aspect is very true and the internet machinery can still attest to that. There is even a moment when in my fishing expedition under disguise I ordered both *The Faint-Hearted Man* and *Scatter The Shrilling Bones* , two of my books, in dollars from Chapter One Books based in Johannesburg.

I even received litigation threats from individuals and families who felt the book passed certain boundaries of not respecting discretion as far as family versus communal archives and records were concerned. Traumatised, I wrote a letter to the publisher explaining the dilemma. They guaranteed me that I was in no danger of any form as I kept potential victims as anonymous as possible in the book itself. However, that would hang over me like a tornado ready to devour me for the rest of my university life. Honestly, I do not know when and where I exactly lifted myself out of that sense of guilt and fear.

Whatever solace the publisher offered never made any sense to me. How I wished that I could just undo the book's publishing process or just tear it into pieces. How I wished I could, in retrospect, kill all the writing instincts in my genes. I guess this could have been one of the factors that contributed to me refusing to write anything while I was at UCT, except for an article, "Your Voice In The Essay" and a poem "In The King Graveyard" published by *Intlola* during my first year at UCT, a student journal published by the UCT department of African Languages & Literature. This essay became very famous with both my lecturers and fellow students that it was "prescribed" in our English for Special Purposes classes to guide students in the art of essay writing. Again, it seemed I could not completely brush up the phenomenon of a rural or urban legend.

For many years to come all I would be was a church orator. Seeking to be relevant, as part of the liturgy, I would do open mic sessions in the local Pentecostal church I attended. As it will be revealed later, that eventually backfired. I also occasionally wrote poems for residence newsletters like the MaquardMask (Leo Marquard Hall) and GSRes (Groote Schuur Residence). Travelling with a taxi from my university residence at Rondebosch, I personally took some of my short stories in English provisionally titled *Flowers For My Mother* to David Phillip Publishers in Claremont. These had been written during my high school days. They were of course rejected, with the same monotonous excuse of "why not consider IsiXhosa publishers?".

I do admit that while at high school my command of the English language was not that great. However, there is no editor in the country who did not know that this young boy "from the Ciskei" heralded from a previously disadvantaged background. I also did send out some few typed poems to the *New Coin* at Rhodes University, a prestigious literary journal edited by one of my high school acquaintances and mentor.

After reading my work and aligning it with poets he knew, one of them being the 17th century classic English poet John Milton, he encouraged me to read a lot. He also sent me a lot of books and journals, some of which were the past editions of *New Coin*. I also attended one of his poetry workshops during the launch of my book at the 1820 Settlers Monument that he had personally organised. Together with the writers' group I had formed while at Kama High School, we travelled to Grahamstown on a mini-bus or taxi that was also organised by him. It would take over three decades for my work to be published in the *New Coin*, obviously under a new editor, Kyle Allan.

MAZRUI'S CULTURAL APPROACH TO UNDERSTANDING PRE- AND POST- COLONIAL AFRICA.

Many arguments have been put forward as an effort to understand the role that Europe has played in Africa; mostly in historically terms. Either way, two terms have been unavoidable: colonization and deconolonization. Different words might have been used interchangeably to capture the impact of Europe in Africa; this is not the point in case for the purposes of this essay. What seems to be of primary importance is the fact that Africa was never the same after its encounter with Europe. For the purposes of this essay two main authors come up, Jaffe (1985) and Mazrui (2005). As the essay question explains, the former offers a political approach to understanding pre- and post- colonial Africa while the latter views this from the cultural angle. The political approach seeks to understand socio-economic institutions and legal frameworks that enabled Africa to operate. The cultural approach looks at all levels of cultures that contributed to the evolution and development of Africa's constituency. The latter, biased towards Mazrui's argument cultural understanding of Africa's evolution will be the main focus of this essay.

In dealing with the essay's main argument, it is of paramount importance to clearly define the different meanings attached to the word Africa, from a historical point

71

of view. This inevitably sets a good background against which Mazrui's argument can be enacted. All the five stages of Africa's evolution, as presented by Mazrui, will be discussed. However, the critical aspects of the essay presupposes a deliberate interjection of thoughts from different authors.

The definition of Africa itself is a contested zone; the name itself exposes Africa to debates about its interaction with other civilisations. Of course, some claim the name "Africa" has got its roots on Berber cultures, whereas some point towards Greco-Roman ancestry. This of course denounces Africa's possible linear journey of evolution solely on the continent's landscape. By all means, this might be pointing towards the possibility of the origin of Mudimbe's thesis, that Africa is a great invention by the imperialist agenda (Mazrui, 2005). There are also debates that the Arabs might have had something to do with the name itself, in terms of *adaptation*. While Europe's conceptualization and cartography of Africa was catastrophic, to the contrary the legacy that Africans (through religion and education) inherited from the Arabs was positive. This then means that "Europe continentalised the African identity".

Right from the onset, it should be made clear that Mazrui chooses to center his argument mainly around two authors, Said and Mudimbe. This is not only because of their preoccupation with *otherness*, which they respectively term *orientalism* and *alterity*. It might be because in them he finds means and ways to chat a way forward for his main thesis.

His is not one single argument *per se* but a programmatic classification of events or stages that he considers very crucial in the evolution of Africa without and within the colonization movement. One should also mention that both Said and Mudimbe attribute their own terms of being to Western imperialism in Africa.

Mazrui, like Mudimbe and Said believe that the post-colonial era is the best time to engage in any studies that seek to debunk colonialism (Mazrui, 2005). They even go further and suggest that even an era preceding colonialism can best be cast in such a manner. Furthermore, it is even better for the subjects of colonialism to interpret their own history and thus seek to "reinvent Africa in their own terms" (Mazrui, 2005:69).

The five stages that Mazrui classifies as Africa's interactive process with the 'other' are as follows: North Africa as an extension of Europe, interactions with the Semitic, classical Greeks and Romans, contacts with Arabs and the spread of Islam, the "triple heritage" and lastly the internationalization of "African glory" (Mazrui, 2005; Alidu, 2014). At a later stage, Mazrui speaks about the dialectics of Africa, still developed along these five stages. Here he highlights five paradoxes that by description fall beyond the scope of this essay. One specific paradox that we are going to deal directly with is what Mazrui call the paradox of history, "that it took Africa's contact with the Arab world to make the Black people of Africa realise that they were black in description, but not necessarily in status" (Mazrui,

2005:70). However, Mazrui does not dismiss the role that Europe played in this debate. He states, "but, on the positive side, it was Europe that continentalized the African identity" (ibid).

Mudimbe, in employing Frobeniun's expressions "African genesis" of 1937 proposes the following steps in the invention and re-invention of Africa, as some sort of an evolutionary process. During the first stage, North Africa was merely conceptualized as an extension of the Mediterranean. Africa's interior "was regarded as an empire of barbarism and darkness" (Mazrui, 2005:70). This was all part of the imperialist, expansionist project (ibid). One cannot understand this debacle without understanding the location of Africa's outside borders (it is Europe again that had the power to conceptualise Africa in terms of boundary creation; land size; typology and names of countries) and within Europe's borders. Therefore, conceptualizing the dynamics of the first stage renders it crucial to understand the whole project of African cartography in the hands of Europe.

The second stage captures Africa as a melting point of many influences; most of which through design or default had these imperial undertones. According to Mazrui (2005), Africa's interaction with the Semitic world, classical Greece and Rome entailed the second phase of the historic conceptualization of Africa. This was a period that entailed not only massive cultural exchange but a systematic repression of the African economy and culture. Of much interest is that these all came carrying the famous "magic bag" of religion and education; old connotations of which are religion and science that Europe utilized to promote its imperialist agendas (Dussel, 2009). The reverse logistics played out by the new export religion promoted these new cultures and systematically erased those of pre-colonial Africa.

The birth of Islam on the Arabian Peninsula would introduce the third phase (Alidu, 2014). As the bearers of this new religion fled for asylum from the great Mecca persecution into Ethiopia this phase would be entrenched. This by all means initiated Africa's continentalisation through the lines of skin color. This "was, in reality, the Sudanisation of sub-Saharan Africa, awakening the people to Black consciousness" (Mazrui, 2005:70). The confluence of Islam and Northern Africa had its complications and challenges. The Islam refugees fled from the great Mecca persecution – only to wage war with other religions in Africa (that of course were not indigenous religions in Africa). Throughout this onslaught driven along the lines of religion, the only Christian church that survived is the Ethiopian Coptic Church, only because at its core it had Byzantine elements that far outlived the Christian religion and whose elements had already been infused into the local version of indigenous knowledge systems long before the arrival of Christianity (Mazrui, 2005; Smith, 2012).

It is at this stage that an antithesis of Europe's version of racism agenda was offered. As Mazrui (2005) illustrates, this on its own became a paradox as it offered Africa's own identity back to Africans – that of Blackness. However, Mazrui is not critical of the methods through which this redemptive tool was offered. Hence, both the gold and the intellect that defined that golden age is part of history now. One could argue that its conception itself was foreign; that is Islam and an education system that maybe came with those refugees who ran from Mecca. At another level, Mazrui fails to acknowledge the role that slavery played in the Islam religion – both at sexual (slaves were bought for sexual purposes) and economic levels (Smith, 2012).

The fourth stage entailed an acknowledgement that three civilisations had converged in a unique development path in Africa (Mazrui, 2005). To some extent, this entailed an awareness of the impact of the spread of Islam in the African continent. During this stage, three civilisations were particularly picked out as responsible: Africanity, Islam and the West (Mazrui, 2005). This would be later termed as "the triple heritage" (ibid). This is the unique African situation whereby through interacting with various civilisations it had been given birth to.

Unfortunately the stage prior to the fourth stage was to be interjected by the impact of Europe's imperialist agendas, and thus directly leading to the fourth stage. Sadly, by the fourth stage, one can sense the pessimistic tone of Mazrui's voice as he enters this contested stage. He talks about, "Europe's capitalist penetration and subsequent colonization" (Mazrui, 2005:68). One could say that the cat in the "magic bag" was rearing its ugly head. It is only late in the process; and the fourth stage of Muzrai development process that this double legacy featured in its own development agenda's within Africa's linear development process (*inter alia* the fact Africa had interacted with other cultures already; the Sematic and the Arabic).

The realization of Africa as a 'cradle for humankind' and the consequent glorification entails its fifth historic conceptualization phase. This euphoria enables a needed transition from "dark continent" to "Garden of Eden". However, the discourse of "underdevelopment" which was highly prized for the enactment of previous phases only casts this new realization under a dark shadow: a true paradox in deed (Alidu, 2014). Through the World Bank international money lending policies that survive to date, it is still the advanced world which dictates what happens in the highly "underdeveloped" Africa.

This last and sad stage – Africa's glorification and consequent globalization - undoes all the good captured in the third stage . As Africa was projected into the world stage, it also meant Africa's glory was being slowly stolen. Resources were amassed and Africa's Indigenous Knowledge Systems were stolen and exported to the West (Smith, 2012). During the golden age of Africa's Timbuktu the dual legacy of Africanity and Islam became intertwined (Mazrui, 2005). This then means that through this interaction the Arabs were able to lift Africa's pedestal to a higher level on its own terms – without Europe's assistance. It was later in the process (stage 4) that I think Europe realised the future benefits of high-jacking this success. The benefits from this calculated move were realised in stage 5 – Africa's globalization. At this stage, still Europe sought to do things on its own terms and modalities. Conversely, this was quite too late in the process as many of Africa's countries had been geared to gain independence from the grips of colonialism – having long aligned themselves through the wider canvass of "Blackness" that the Arabs, through Islam and their education had offered long ago.

It is interesting to note that the "dual culture" of religion and education highly praised by Mazrui and brought by Islam into Africa (as experimented in the ancient city of Timbuktu) was itself a remnant of Europe's colonial legacy in the earlier enlightenment project whereby, as Dussel (2009) exposes, religion and science were used as tools to conquer and rule. As the above author argues, too much violence was inherent in Europe's saviour complex (that in psychoanalytic terms that could amount to a certain level of split personality) – which aspect was played out very well in Africa. The double agenda of critiquing religious practices within Africa was not conversely done with enlightenment – they never questioned their own religious practices (Dussel, 2009). This applies to all the three main players then; the Jewish, Christian and consequently the 'hybrid' civilization of Islam.

Long before Europe's own version of modernity, Northern Africa in particular had a duality of civilisations: indigenous

African cultures and Islam (Mali and Songhai) until the Moroccan invasion of 1588-1591. This alone confirms the fact that pre-modern Africa had its own versions of conflict dynamics of which were a result of greediness. As Mazrui states, the "Sudanisation of West Africa linked Islam and Blackness" (Mazrui, 2005:71). The city of Timbuktu was a byproduct of this interaction ("God, gold and glory"). It is through the exotic name of the city that North Africa entered the core of orientalism; and still at another level Africa was being reinvented (Mazrui, 2005). Two overlapping imperial periods of Songhai (1325 – 1591) and Mali (1100 – 1700) defines the coverage of Timbuktu's golden age. Mazrui does not entertain this confluence of periods and cultures and hidden meanings or implications thereof. What socio-political dynamics could have defined this period of overlaps? Could these unexplained moments be attributed to the final downfall of this golden era? The fusion of Blackness and Islam is treated and presented in very simplistic manners. What about those religions that pre-existed Islam in this region of Africa? To what extent was Islam used as both a tool to create subjects and to enforce ideology? As already hinted, what role did slavery play in the domination of Islam? To some extent, Mazrui (2005) hints that these links defined periods of hostility and greed (for example, the Moroccan invasion of 1588 – 1591).

Mazrui proudly declares Timbuktu was one point of the triology of Black academic excellence; two of which are Al-Azhar University in Cairo and Qarawiyin University in Morocco. He also declares that Al-Azhar is the oldest university in the world; covering almost a millennium. In my own understanding, the modern version of Timbuktu could be articulated as visiting professorships, sabbaticals, academic chairs and the actual physical outputs as in format of academic journals. This could be true, as Mazrui states that these three ancient universities were interdependent. During those days, "blackness was recognised as compatible with excellence" (Mazrui, 2005:72).

In conclusion, Jaffe (1985) and Mazrui's (2005) semantics on the route that Africa took after its encounter with Europe have been indispensable in Africa's post-colonial studies. The present essay has focused on Mazrui's contribution in the contribution of Islam, most notable the Arabs in not only Africa's pigmentation but its progress in term of scholarly achievements. Through introducing North Africa to the Arabic civilization, Europe's contribution to Africa, besides colonial and humiliation attempts, was an awareness of Blackness. Along with this awareness, the Islam education system has been of lasting contribution not only to Northern Africa but to the whole of Africa. Hence the term, "Europe's continentalisation of Africa" (Mazrui, 2005). The direct engagement with Mazrui's text has seen the essay going through the five stages of Africa's encounter with Europe. These are: North Africa as an extension of Europe, interactions with the Semitic, classical Greeks and Romans, contacts with Arabs and the spread of Islam, the "triple heritage" and lastly the internationalization of "African glory" (Mazrui, 2005; Alidu, 2014). At a later stage, Mazrui speaks about the dialectics of Africa, still developed along these five stages. To him, these entail Africa's five paradox. These are: "paradox of the "Garden of Eden" in decay, paradox of "humiliation", paradox of "clash of civilisation", paradox of "underdevelopment", paradox of "size" and paradox of "physical location" in the globe (Alidu, 2014). For the purposes of this essay, the latter were not discussed.

BIBLIOGRAPHY:

Alidu, 2014. "Conflict and Society in Africa Session 1: Nature of African Societies. Political Studies Lecture. University of Ghana.

Ashcroft. B. et al. 1989. Routledge: New York. The Empire Writes Back

Dussel, E. 2009. A New Age In The History Of Philosophy. The World Dialogue Between Philosophical Traditions. *Philosophy And Social Criticism,* 35(5): 499-516.

Jaffe, H. 1985. African communism and despotism. In Jaffe, H. *A History of Africa*: London: Zed. pp. 5-40.

Jaffe, H. 1985. European Colonialism. In Jaffe, H. *A History Of Africa*. London: Zed. pp. 41-68.

Mazrui, A. 2005. The Re-invention of Africa: Edward Said, V.Y. Mudimbe, and Beyond. *Research in African Literatures.* 36(3), Edward Said, Africa and Cultural Criticism. pp. 68-82.

Smith, L.T. 2012. Zed Books: London & New York. Imperialism, History And Theory (In Smith, L.T. *Decolonising Methodologies.*

THE CLEANSING RITUAL

There is an African saying, "You have to mutter a word before entering someone's household" (Ubodumzela xa ungena komny'umzi). This saying is used in songs sung by the elders, both men and women, not only at a young man's circumcision homecoming celebration but also in other traditional ceremonies. The amaXhosa of the Eastern Cape, besides possessing a shrewd ability of coining and preserving wise words that speak directly to matters of social significance, they also are great composers. Besides demanding respect, humility seems to be the living spirit behind this line.

In the same vein, the African Independent Churches demand that every member of the church conducts their own cleansing ritual by throwing whatever is in their hands into a bigger circle of things before the service begins, as a way of greeting the spirit. This simple act also demands that individuals verbally confess all their weekly personal misdemeanours. To speak directly to the occasion, there are chosen songs and portions of the church liturgy in form of Psalms from the now historically conflated Hebraic and Hellenic traditional texts.

In a more traditional setting, the singing of "Nomame", the most sacred song as far as the amaXhosa tradition and cosmology is concerned, demands that elders should confess all their sins of omission as far as offerings are concerned. This is done up to a point of discrediting the living patriarchal lineage and their "silent" forbears for the sake of appeasing the lion spirit. That is just before entering the African kraal as one, in full awe of the spirits, holds the venerated spear. The belief is that directly addressing the ancestors, who also happen to be gatekeepers, will not only clear the way for the heifer or bull of sacrifice but is a cleansing opportunity for every member of the particular clan.

Even the most feared and respected *sanuse*, chief *sangoma,* sings appeasing songs to the different spirits claimed by the mountains, forests, caves, rivers and oceans. He/she not only addresses the guardian spirits by name but offers gifts to them. After many twilights in my life, what else can I do but come in full circle. As I enter the sacred place, in full murmur, this is my own cleansing ritual. The space is not mine; it belongs to the elders.

II

It is approximately thirty years ago and my time to 'ascend the mountain' has finally come. My family is very nervous about the whole affair, as in the past few years the soon to be *umkhwetha* had courted other identities. As a young boy evangelist, I had clearly communicated my ideas of what I thought about the *amaXhosa* tradition of male circumcision. Manhood, the idea which this rite of passage encapsulated, could never be validated in this event - so I wanted to believe. As a born again Christian and a second year student in the University of Cape Town, I thought I had carved my *identity* elsewhere.

I hated tradition. My religious environment taught me to hate tradition; African customs. I was discouraged from understanding the dynamics behind whatever the African people whose culture (which was mine also) demanded as more than a way of life. I failed to understand the analogy of the ancestors and the consequent meaning that this symbolism has for those who are alive. I failed to see the meanings that the African people attach to their own spiritual world. So, even though I did end up being circumcised, I refused to partake in any sacrifice; or any form of activity that was tagged "ancestor worship" by my religious circle. I refused to eat the right shoulder of a goat, *umngcamlo*, that is part of going through the initiation rite.

I had decided to give my own spiritual energies to a foreign God I had embraced as part of my conversion to a new tradition; that of Christ and his followers. Just after my religious conversion I had also undergone another significant transition, securing a place of study at a historically white university - the University of Cape Town. These two incidents offered me valid reasons to aspire to a new identity, a perfect antithesis to what I was and surprisingly what (to my late discovery) I would always be.

Ironically, though, I started to become obsessed by my project of detesting tradition. As an unintended consequence, my own detestation of tradition started shifting away from that of the ancestor forms of worship that the African community (a clearly identifiable enemy, according to my religious inclinations) obviously offered. I started hating anything that smacked of any form of tradition, be it African religion or not. With the lack of a suitable word, I also started questioning Christian symbolism and worship. The academic environment also lost the appeal it initially bore for the intellectual novice that I was before I arrived at UCT for my first year of study. I started losing faith in everything that I had formerly attached value to.

III

Possessed with feelings of antagonism I reluctantly consented to undergo the process of initiation, a moment that would define the course of my life. My family had the upper-hand. Against my will, as custodians of the rite of male circumcision, they insisted on brewing the traditional beer and slaughtering the goat to prepare for my "getting-in" ritual or *umngeno*. As my faith was grounded elsewhere, I refused to partake in any of these proceedings. Now that I had agreed to be circumcised, I just wanted my circumcision to be as simple as possible.

A week just before this ritual, I refused to perform the last dance with my initiation cohorts. Nevertheless, they received all their entitlements; food, traditional beer and even the highly prized "bottle of the horn" – *ibhotile yephondo* . On a Friday afternoon, a day just before the *ingcibi* would use the traditional weapon, *umdlanga* to perform the surgical operation the medicated right shoulder of the sacrificial goat (*umngcamlo*) was eaten on my behalf by one of my many cousins or sisters. This was just after my head was shaved; the first mark towards this journey of transition. I did not spend all the prescribed three weeks in the mountain. Instead, after undergoing a lot of stress and imagining that some people were practicing witchcraft on me, I summoned an ambulance and went to recover at S.S. Gida hospital in Keiskammahoek, a rural small town few kilometres from home.

At some point, I had to leave the born-again Christian church I belonged to as it could no longer accommodate the "prophet" I was quickly becoming. In fact, after spending nearly a decade there, the pastor of this mostly "coloured" church in Cape Town summoned me to the cry room and said, "Brother Isaac, I think you should start your own church". This would be the beginning of a completely new journey for me, back to the African roots of my Eastern Cape childhood.

Instead of "starting my own church" I returned to the Methodist church where I had grown up. There I quickly progressed to the point of registering for studies to train as a minister. This was while I was working in Pretoria for Statistics South Africa. Before I could sit for my first exams, I could feel that 'cry room moment' approaching again. So I prepared for it by summoning the elders and telling them of my new challenge – the calling from the ancestors to be a *sangoma*. They were very supportive. They relinquished me "to do what was right" with the proviso that once everything was settled I should come back home again.

Instead, the road unwounded to unexpected possibilities. The cry room "prophecy" was finally fulfilled as I ended up starting my own church after I shadowed within the African Independent faith healing church (of St John's Faith Mission that was founded by Christina Nku in 1906). The late Archbishop Fihla was my mentor. At the same time, within a lot of pain and doubt, I was also growing as a *sangoma* up to a point that I started practicing. I am a ventriloquist who uses both the Bible and oracle cards to dig into people's pasts, present and futures. For personal purposes, I also occasionally throw bones. I translate some of these 'rare moments' into poems that not only offer personal healing but also serve as media through which I transverse alternative worlds of thought. My Master of Arts thesis in Creative Writing at the University of Cape Town owes its existence and success to such moments.

I dig herbs that sometimes come through my dreams. I use the media of the mountain, forest, cave, river and the ocean to assist people to embrace both their healing and spiritual completeness. The vibration of certain crystals complements some of my healing activities.

However, another moment would push my "rolling stone" life towards another direction. I started having dreams about spears and sacred herbs. One aspect of this is presiding over family traditional functions through assisting with the bellowing of the heifer or bull of sacrifice. Around 2010 I performed my first of these kind of functions within the blessings of the patrilineal Nkabane clan. Another aspect is presiding over traditional male initiation functions. This has not yet been resolved as I myself doubt my manhood within the amaXhosa context, considering the direction that my own traditional initiation function took. Still, this has led to another aspect, a research interest in the area of traditional male circumcision and indigenous knowledge systems.

LOVE BASILS

My argument is based on the book of Esther, a young Jewish woman of note who not only uses her beauty, splendor and intelligence to attract a very powerful Gentile king but puts her life in extreme danger to save her own people. If I would have a focal point, it would be based on the Biblical book of Esther 2:9. Before going into my topic, which revolves around the ritual cleansing of Esther before she is presented before the ruling monarch of the then Persian diaspora, let me say a little about the background of Esther's story.

The story of Esther portrays an unexpected journey of love between Esther and a very powerful Persian king. Esther is the daughter of Abihail, the uncle of Mordecai. At the time of the narration of the story she is already an orphan and is under Mordecai's custodianship. According to the book of Esther (Esth. ii. 5-7, 15), Mordecai had previously been carried into captivity together with Jeconiah by Nebuchadnezer, King of Babylon.

In Esther's story, the *supportive* protagonist is Ahasuerus, or Xerxes I, a Persian king who ruled "from India even unto Ethiopia, over an hundred and seven and twenty provinces" - that is, over the Achaemid Empire. Some sources state that there is no reference to known historical events in the story; the narrative of *Esther* was invented to provide an aetiology for Purim, and the name Ahasuerus is usually understood to refer to a fictionalized Xerxes I, who ruled the Achaenid Empire between 486 and 465 BCE.

To further place the story of Esther in the realms of legend there are also claims that Persian kings did not marry outside a restricted number of Persian noble families. Considering this historical fact, it is thus impossible that there was a Jewish queen Esther. The proponents of this argument claim that instead the historical Xerxes's queen was Amestris. Nevertheless, the Holy Bible (KJV) states, "So Esther was taken unto king Ahasuerus into his house royal in the tenth month, which is the month Tebeth, in the seventh year of his reign" (Esther 2:16).

It must be highlighted that the King James Version identifies this king as Ahasuerus, and that is the identification I am going to stick with. As stated by some sources, numerous scholars have proposed theories as to who Ahasuerus represents. It is furthermore stated that most scholars generally identify him with Xerxes I, as did 19th-century Bible commentaries.-As revealed by the above mentioned sources, three factors, among others, contribute to this identification:

1. It is agreed the Hebrew 'Ahasuerus' descended from the Persian names for Xerxes.
2. Historian Herodotous views Xerxes I as being susceptible to women and in the habit of making extravagant offers to them, just as he did to Esther ("up to half my kingdom"). Herodotus mentions

that the Persian empire stretched from India to Ethiopia and also refers to the magnificent royal palace in Shushan, corroboration of what is stated in the Book of Esther. In addition Herodotus mentions an assembly of Persian nobles called by Xerxes to advise him on the proposed war against Greece. Although Herodotus does not give the location of this assembly, the date - "after Egypt was subdued" - corresponds to Xerxes' third year when Esther records an assembly of Persian nobility at a feast. (Histories VII.8) Herodotus also mentions that following his defeat at Salamis Xerxes I became involved in harem intrigues involving his wife Amestris and his daughter-in-law, with whom he became enamoured. (Histories IX.108) Herodotus relates this occurred in the tenth month of his seventh year as king — the same time Ahasuerus was choosing beautiful women for his harem (Esther 2:16).

3 Annals from the reign of Xerxes I mention an otherwise unattested official by the name of "Marduka", which some have proposed refers to Mordecai, as both are mentioned serving in the king's court.

However trivial the story of Esther is treated by some, there are those who take the Biblical presentation as historical facts. To the latter, the account is given, "in the biblical book named after her, Esther is a young Jewish woman living in the Persian diaspora who finds favor with the king, becomes queen, and risks her life to save the Jewish people from destruction when the court official Haman persuades the king to authorize a pogrom against all the Jews of the empire. Written in the diaspora in the late Persian/early Hellenistic period (fourth century B.C.E.), the Book of Esther is a Jewish novella that deals with the enduring issues of preserving Jewish identity and ensuring survival amid cultural pressures and hostile enemies in a foreign land".

The story goes, that in the third year of his reign, king Ahasuerus made a great feast in his royal palace at Shushan. This lasted for 180 days. As stated in the Holy Bible, "On the seventh day, when the heart of the king was merry with wine, he commanded Mehuman, Biztha, Harbona, Bigtha, and Abagtha, Zethar, and Carcas, the seven chamberlains that served in the presence of Ahasuerus the king, to bring Vashti the queen before the king with the crown royal, to shew the people and the princes her beauty: for she was fair to look on". (Esther 1:10-11). As the queen was busy enjoying a beauty contest amongst women from all her kingdoms in the palace right under the nose of the king, she refused to come before him. The king was thus very furious and sought advice from his wise counsel. The men who sat before him clearly put it as the king is a man of great power and whose kingdom stretches over a large territory of land; this certainly sets a wrong precedent. Even more, men will be able to rule over their households. Thus, they advised the king to dispose Vashti from the throne.

Without further delays, let us move to the protagonist of the story, who is Esther. A call was made throughout the then Persian diaspora to bring all beautiful women to the palace so the king can choose a wife. Mordecai, under disguise, decided to bring Esther into the palace to also be part of the contest. As soon as she was brought in, the chamberlain, keeper of the women, was very much pleased with Esther. The Holy Bible states, "And the maiden pleased him, and she obtained kindness of him; and he speedily gave her things for purification, with such things as belonged to her, and seven maidens, which were meet to be given her, out of the king's house: and he preferred her and her maids unto the best place of the house of the women" (Esther 2:9).

Before being presented to the king, the women were required to undergo a rigorous cleansing ritual, which lasted for almost a year:

Now when every maid's turn was come to go in to king Ahasuerus, after that she had been twelve months, according to the manner of the women, (for so were the days of their purifications accomplished, to wit, six months with oil of myrrh, and six months with sweet odours, and with other things for the purifying of the women;)

Then thus came every maiden unto the king; whatsoever she desired was given her to go with her out of the house of the women unto the king's house.

In the evening she went, and on the morrow she returned into the second house of the women, to the custody of Shaashgaz, the king's chamberlain, which kept the concubines: she came in unto the king no more, except the king delighted in her, and that she were called by name (Esther 2: 12-14).

Now, we have arrived to the climax of my argument. What is a basil? A basil is any form of aromatic plant. The computerised thesaurus I have just consulted lists the following under the name basil: herb; rosemary; sage; thyme; parsley. These are all sacred plants. In IsiXhosa, my vernacular, we would put all the above under the category of *ubulawu*. *Ubulawu* are sacred plants not only used to facilitate communication with the ancestors but also for *cleansing*. There is a certain category of *ubulawu* which is solely for women who desire to get married. For now, I will not go into detail with that. The only thing I can say is that to specialised individuals or shamans, these are easily accessible. They can be accessed as far as in the forests of Limpopo and as close to my backyard at both my rural Eastern Cape maternal and paternal rural homes.

As a minor divergence to the main topic, let me also mention this point. Remember, way down in history, outside the territories of bondage and slavery, another Jew was presented with one of these sacred herbs at birth. We all know the story. Jesus Christ was given myrrh as one of his gifts. For now, I do not have time and space to discuss the significance of this gift and its possible links with the story of Esther. All I can say is that the symbolism of the king's golden sceptre that he had lifted in recognition of Esther was being passed on (Esther 5:2).

Now, let us go back to the character of Esther. The only thing I would like to dig into now to illustrate my point is the meaning of her name. Close readers of the Bible will know that Esther is not the real of this future queen. Mordecai, in fear of victimisation, did not divulge her real Persian name (for she was the lineage of those who were left behind in captivity and had to bear a Persian name). Her real name is Hadassah. The English meaning of this name is Myrtle. One source identifies a myrtle as "any of the *evergreen shrubs in the genus Myrtus,* belonging to the family Myrtaceae. ... In Greco-Roman antiquity, the common myrtle was held to be sacred to Venus and was used as an emblem of love in wreaths and other decorations". Quite an interesting coincidence indeed. The fruit, leaves, and branches are used to make medicine.

Another source further states, "its aroma has been described as that *of a lemon lolly, perfumed with menthol notes.* We harvest the plants for their lemon myrtle leaves, which release this strong scent when crushed. The plant's sweet citrus aroma comes from its natural compounds - citral, citronellal, and linalool". Interesting! Lastly, the same source states, "the myrtle is not mentioned in the Bible until the time of the captivity. The first reference is in Nehemiah 8:15 in regard to the celebration of the Feast of Tabernacles. ... As an evergreen, fragrant shrub associated with watercourses, the myrtle *is a fitting symbol of the recovery and establishment of God's promises."* I would not like to say anymore as the above mentioned quotations are self-explanatory. It took an intense connection with sacred herbs for a period of a year for Esther to capture this very powerful Gentile king. Furthermore, within Esther was wrapped God's promises to save and restore His people.

I would like to conclude this argument with the following note. Overall, what do we learn from the Book of Esther? As young people from different walks of life, we all have a divine purpose. It rests upon us to allow God to assist us to find that purpose. It might be within your family, it might be within your immediate community, it might be at a national level. But the purpose is there and it is staring right at your eyes. Unequivocally so, as one source reveals:

Like the books of Daniel or Tobit, the Book of Esther raises questions about how to live as a Jew in diaspora. However, the Book of Esther is unique in two important respects. First, although Mordecai has an important role and finishes the story at a very high rank, it is ultimately Esther, a woman, who saves her people. This choice of a female hero serves an important function in the story. Women were, in the world of the Persian diaspora as in many other cultures, essentially powerless and marginalized members of society. Even if they belonged to the dominant culture, they could not simply reach out and grasp power, as a man could; whatever power they could obtain was earned through the manipulation of the public holders of power, men. In this sense the Jew living in a foreign land could identify with the woman: he or she too was essentially powerless and marginalized, and power could be obtained only through one's wits and talents. But, as the actions of Esther demonstrate, this can be done. By astutely using her beauty, charm, and political intelligence, and by taking one well-placed risk, Esther saves her people, brings about the downfall of their enemy, and elevates her kinsman to the highest position in the kingdom. Esther becomes the model for the Jew living in diaspora or exile.

UNDER THE SHADOW OF A BAOBAB TREE

They sit under the big shadow of a baobab tree with their legs wide open. The chief circumciser, a respected man in the village, moves upside down singing inconceivable chants as if to scare them. His assistants make sure that every -*bijii* is correctly placed so they could be properly cut by the traditional surgeon. Are they scared? The traditional assegai that will soon consume their prepuces is the only thing they need to transform the dreaded -*bijii* that they are to the status of the *nthaka* that they have always desired since the day they became aware of their sexuality. In between sterilisation of the traditional weapon in the traditional beer, the chief circumciser – together with his assistants- quickly run through the operation like a bolt of lightening. The echoes declaring the achievement of a new status run up to the women, children, uncircumcised boys and strangers in the far away village who are forbidden to witness such occasions. In tandem, they celebrate. Everybody celebrates.

This happens after a two-year waiting period after which they underwent a pre-circumcision ritual. This is where through a medium of local mythology and tribal legends they were sworn to a vow of secrecy. The Tharaka, "part of the larger Ameru Bantu ethnic group who occupy the Tharaka Nithi County in the Eastern slopes of Mount Kenya which is located about 300 kilometres from the city of Nairobi"[9] are one of the African tribes who though negatively dealt by British colonialism still value their cultures. Traditional male circumcision is one those cultures that although have been almost wiped out by "civilisation" have managed to exist parallel with "modern" forms of male circumcision.

The *kirimo*-swallowing ritual, whereby each candidate is ushered from junior boyhood -*mwiji* to senior boyhood or circumcision candidate -*rugu* takes place in the solace and the mystique of Mount Kenya. Besides the veil of secrecy embedded in the ritual, candidates are prepared to be strong warriors and responsible owners of land, property and women. After the long-winded ritual, they get sent back to the village, with a quasi-new status of course. This is because after roughly a period of two years they still have to under-go circumcision which this process was preparing them for.

The first male circumcision to take place in a hospital setting in Kenya was in 1929, at Chogoria Mission Hospital. From the focal point of Marimanti District where this hospital is located, this new kind of circumcision disseminated to almost all districts of rural Kenya. This was popular amongst

---

[9] Moywaywa, C.K. & Akaranga, S.I. (2017). Pre-modern and Modern Male Circumcision Rites among the Tharaka of Eastern Kenya. Journal of Education & Enterpreneurship. 4(10) 48 – 59.

the highly educated and Christians. This was when new circumcision calendars were introduced, as opposed to the indigenous knowledge-based (that most of the times were linked to honouring ancient African gods) festivals that took place in the villages.

As convenient as this new circumcision method sounds, it had its own challenges. As it was directly linked to school calendars, boys who did not perform well at schools were literally left behind. This directly resulted into psycho-social challenges. As traditional male circumcision still continues up to date, the former also presents a cultural conflict of some kind. To mitigate these challenges, a certain kind of a compromise had to be reached. As opposed to those circumcisions that happened completely in hospitals (in terms of candidates also recovering in hospitals); there was also an option where initiates could be outpatients. The latter allowed for the traditional method still to be integrated within this new "modern" way of circumcision. Also, the inmates were denied certain types of visitors who were viewed as "impure" and still allowed a traditional "crash course" in hospital. How these two methods were successfully in mitigating cultural stigma on those who went through the "modern" route is still a story for another day.

Looking at how the story of male circumcision has evolved in the Eastern Cape Province of South Africa since the two centuries of recorded history, one would vow that there were cultural exchanges between these two African regions. Excluding the mandatory *kirimo*- swallowing ritual two years prior the actual three–four weeks circumcision ritual in Kenya, every other stage is a carbon stage of the other. One would safely argue that in the case of the Eastern Cape amaXhosa the former was tightly integrated with the latter in formative times as initiation candidates used to spend in excess of six months in the bush.

The impact of missionary funded education and Christianity has also had its effects in the Eastern Cape Province TMC practices up to a point that at a certain group of amaXhosa not only called for its modernization but also for its complete abolition. Taking into consideration the high rates of both initiate morbidity and mortality, academics and activists questioned the authenticity of the custom. For a lack of a most competent word, the media also played a prominent role in exposing these cultural ineptitudes. This opened an argument for the possibility of introducing Voluntary Medical Male Circumcision (VMMC) not only as a safe haven against initiate morbidity and mortality but as a possibility of preventing sexual transmitted diseases like HIV/AIDS. Of course, some amaXhosa traditional loyalists like Prince Zolile Burns-Ncamashe would not take that with arms folded.

PALM PRAYER

I wondered what my grandfather did with palm twigs, he sent me away every sun-rise, he gave me a small sack, with clear instructions on what to collect. Accompanied by an army of dogs owned by my grand-father, I would invade the little patch of forest just a stone-throw away from our village home. Coming back home, I would be instructed to leave them at the wide entrance to the kraal, a home to our many beasts and chicken. The latter, they loved to sleep on top of the kraal's roof. My grand-father said it was imperative that the palm twigs be kissed by the stoic Qamata before his already creased hands touched them.

My child mind also wondered and wondered, he could read my young mind, and whenever he could he provided me with answers, no matter how enigmatic they were to me. He would tell me that sleeping in the kraal's many rooms is the long line of forebears who he owed allegiance to. These forebears owed allegiance to an unseen God, Qamata. My young mind would not bear the significance of a graceful Qamata sitting somewhere above the picturesque sun-shades, owing to my Sunday school teachings that pointed to a bigger God residing somewhere in the skies.

I have already alluded to the fact that my grandfather was more than a mind reader, so he would go on explaining that Qamata pre-existed the Sunday school God. Immediately after dropping the palm twigs at the kraal's entrance I would run away from my grandfather's sight to embrace the youthful circle of the day. This involved a long list of games; games that never provided us with any food to eat, and also nothing to drink. At the merciless hands of hunger we would all retreat to our homes scattered throughout the mountain village. On my arrival at home, a long que of people would be waiting outside the yard to see my grandfather. I told you, my grandfather's eye could see everywhere.

They came to seek out his enduring wisdom. I would sit next to him, with my arms folded. In his divinations, he held his flywhisk with such confidence, like a priest of an ancient God, maybe Qamata, whose mission was to leave no stone unturned. I loved my grand-father, especially when he was caught up in that spiral of thought that defined his onuses. He would tell his visitors everything they needed to know, especially the part they loved the most, the reason why they left their village homes to come and seek his advice I never thought a normal human being could do such extrapolations that is why I venerated my grandfather. He would then give each of his visitors a leaf from the palm twigs he sent me to pick up from Hlathikhulu.

Depending on the predictions from the oracle custodian and ventriloquists housed inside the white beaded calabashes - my grandfather's guide - he would open up a goat-skin bag and prescribe medication. Also, some of them would call him to their compounds for further rituals. He never asked anyone to accompany him on these night journeys. This particular day, he requested me to prepare his goat-skin bag that he used to carry along. With such pride, I moved up and down the big compound my grand-father owned before the Trust Laws that dwindled our people's properties to nothing came into effect.

With his long tobacco pipe bursting from his mouth, he sent many confusing commands to my young mind. I was precise, so I thought. After I had counted every head of my grandfather's many goats, my only responsibility at that age, he summoned me to his *ndumba*, or small hut. He took out a small bag made out of an animal skin, maybe a springbok. Slowly his already creased hands opened it. With one blow from his mouth he gushed out so much air into this bag and he threw the contents into a small grass mat in-front of him. He shook his head, then blew again. He pointed to the scattered bones with his divining stick or flywhisk, again with such poise and gracefulness. Voices grumbled from his stomach. He shook his head. He put the contents back to the small bag and put it to his goat-skin bag. He asked me to carry the venerated goat-skin bag and there we hit the darkened goat paths of the mountainous terrain that was our home.

In his hands he carried his flywhisk, a branch from the palm tree twigs, a home-made torch and his wild olive knob-kirrie. In full circle, following the pattern of the mud rondavel, his hosts were silently waiting. On our arrival one of them, presumably the head of the clan, retrieved the palm tree leaf from a grass ceiling and put it next to the fire smoke-darkened pillar. My grandfather laid his belongings next to the palm tree leaf. Without saying anything he took out the contents of the goat-skin bag and laid them on top of the palm tree leaves. The rest cannot be narrated, still in its clandestine nature, left incisions in my young mind that have subsisted even up to date as I follow on my grand-father's giant footsteps.

THE MISSIONARY

My whole journey to be a minister is a haunting reminder of the destructive forces that have torn apart my community and consequently my own family. What is sad is that it seems I am alone in this road of discovery. Even my own family, servants of the church, seems to be blind to this truth. The theological centre at Salem that they whisked me to resonates with the painful legacy of colonialism, oppression and internalised self-hatred that has led to brother turning against brother, sister against sister and child against parent. In this moment, I realise that the journey to reclaim my ancestorial heritage is not only about celebrating my roots but also about confronting the painful truths of my history. In my own terms, I must face the ways in which the oppressive forces of colonialism and systematic racism have fractured my community and my own sense of self.

From a position and angle of spiritual seeking and intellectual pursuits, I am now displaced from the very institution that was supposed to nurture my growth. The theological centre, once a beacon of knowledge and faith, has become a symbol of rejection and exclusion. My displacement serves as a poignant reminder that the journey to reclaim my ancestral heritage and cultural identity is not without its challenges and sacrifices. The contrast between the oppressive forces of colonialism and my own convictions could not be more stark. My only comfort lies in the fact that as I leave the theological centre behind, I carry with me the wisdom of my forebears and the knowledge gleaned from my investigative journey. Hopefully, I am now poised to forge a new path, one that reconciles my faith with my cultural identity and ancestral heritage.

My mental health suffered, and I found myself in a local hospital, struggling to cope with the conflicting demands of my identity. This painful and vulnerable moment in my story highlighted the devastating consequences of colonialism's legacy which forced individuals to choose between their ancestral heritage and the imposed beliefs of their oppressors. At that point in time, it was my distant wish to begin to reconcile my dual identities and find a path that honoured both my ancestors and my personal convictions.

The theological school's strict policies and isolation from external influences only added to my feelings of disconnection and confinement. The prohibition of "heathen beliefs" and the restriction on vacations and visitors created a sense of cultural and spiral suffocation, making it difficult for me to connect with my ancestral heritage. This environment, intended to shape me into a devout follower, instead fuelled my inner turmoil. The suppression of my true self and the erasure of cultural identity threatened to consume me. My ancestors' whispers, though muted, still lingered, refusing to be silenced.

The darkness of doubt and uncertainty enveloped me. The theological school's rigid dogma and the suppression of my ancestral heritage had led me to a crisis of identity. The sentry words from Mr Sunhill, the first principal of the seminary, just before I departed from the seminary haunted me:

Remember that your ancestral spirits and your calling as a healer are still part of you, even if you have passed theological studies. You can integrate these aspects of yourself and find a way to reconcile your past, present and future. Integrating your experiences and callings means finding ways to harmonize your ancestral spirits, healing abilities, theological education and personal connections. Integration is a personal and ongoing process. Be kind to yourself.

II

By the way, I have not yet narrated my story. All this has just been a prelude. Born at the Nqabara constellation of villages, with an average elevation of 1.312 feet above sea level, I grew up along the West Coast shaded by a girdle of indigenous bush. This picture of a sense and picturesque childhood, nestled in the heart of nature, grounds in a specific time and place which is the pre-colonial epoch and unspoilt natural sanctuaries. As broken the umbilical cord of my past is, I still desired the tranquillity and connection to the natural world. Offering protection and continuous embrace, the natural world cradled me as I grew up. Indeed , the cultural and geographical context of my upbringing's rich heritage and environment was unique. I reiterate myself, the soothing umbilical cord was long broken!

Under present day demarcation rules, my home village directly falls within the boundaries of Mbashe Local Municipality. Surrounded by the four nature reserves of Dwesa, Hluleka, Silaka and Mkambathi, its shoulders leaned more on the Dwesa game reserve. This is where nature and game reserves converged with the Indian Ocean's majestic sweep. Like a permutation of about a millenary of pythons, the Indian Ocean – adding a sense of scope and connection to the broader region - spiralled through these strikingly beautiful landscapes and watercourses towards Kwazulu - Natal. This further conveys the dynamic and serpentine movement of the ocean's waters. This is also testament to the power of the language of this enchanting stretch of land and coastline to evoke the beauty and wonder of our world.

Along the strategically dotted beach-line, routinely sleeping, that sometimes looked like an amphitheatre, were Cintsa, Mazeppe Bay, Coffee Bay and Port St John's main-lands. The famous pink waters of the Sinuka, a direct cousin of the great Mzimvubu River, that gushed endlessly from the heart of this coastal landscape was also a healing gift to this beautiful and holy stretch of land. As if in unison, they all kissed the mouth of these blue camouflaged waters with such vigour and consistency. These paint a picture of a breath-taking landscape, where the beach-line is dotted with picturesque towns and bays, resembling an amphitheatre. The metaphor of the lands kissing the ocean waters with vigour and steadiness creates a sense of harmony and unity between the natural elements. This distinct and varied panorama, with all its unspoilt natural glory, seems to be composing a love letter to this beautiful and holy land.

Like sentient beings absorbed in a solemn summit, a number of trees reverently stood along the coastline. Depending on the swinging moods of the bipolar-weather that defined this thematic coastline, these trees sometimes bowed their heads, sometimes shook their entire bodies and sometimes lifted their many miniature hands. The above mentioned weather, which governs the trees' movements, adds a sense of drama and unpredictability, while the nod to the creatures that call the ocean home acknowledges the interconnectedness of the ecosystem. The image of the trees forming a formidable fort, separating the mainland from the vast Indian Ocean creates a sense of protection and boundary. It is as if the trees are guardians of the ocean's secrets, standing watch over the ever-changing tides.

All this done just at the right time and moment, as if to pay homage not only to the massive waters but to the creatures whose home are these blue-carpeted waters. If I could name but a few: the milkwood, the wild camphor bush, the coast silver oak, the New Zealand Christmas tree and the Norfolk pine - all formed a formidable fort partly separating the mainland from those deep and endless waters of the quivering Indian Ocean.

The milkwood tree, a majestic giant, stood as a sentinel, providing shelter and shade for various village activities. It was a hub of community life, hosting imbizos (gatherings), makeshift schools, and halls. For me and my fellow children, it was a playground, a haven for laughter and adventure. The numerous other trees, a veritable sanctuary, played a vital role in the village's well-being. They harboured the indigenous healers, revered for their wisdom and knowledge, snowballed down through generations.

These 'native doctors' were not only esteemed locally but also sought after by communities from afar. They were kingmakers, their influence extending beyond the village borders. It is very important to poignantly highlight the significance of these trees, which have been the backbone of the community's existence, especially during times of austerity. The trees have been a constant, a symbol of resilience and strength, providing shelter, sustenance, and healing. At another level, one has to conjure up words to pay tribute to the enduring spirit of the village and the ancient wisdom that reside within its people and the land itself.

As it was during the days of the most powerful and omnipresent medicine man *baba* uKgotso Sethuntsa, local chiefs, kings and politicians lingered here for both coronation, or *ukugcotywa*, and protection. The fact that local chiefs and politicians seek coronation and protection at this sacred site underscores the enduring importance of tradition and spiritual guidance in the lives of leaders and communities. We were told by elders that there is nothing strange or peculiar about this practice as from time immemorial not only our system of governance but average men and women utilised these sacred services to be entrenched into the wider society. The story of the very famous medicine man whose many patrons speckled the endless corridors of state power during the time of Paul Kruger, as he himself was a devote follower of *baba* uKgotso, will always assume life within the invisible pages of both African folklore and urban legend. The above mentioned scenario suggests a sense of continuity, as if the legacy of Baba Kgotso Sethuntsa still resonates in this place, where the past and present converge.

The elders' wisdom provides context and depth to the practice, revealing roots in ancient tradition and cultural significance. The notion that both governance and everyday people have sought these sacred services to integrate into society highlights the importance of spirituality in African culture. These all become a fascinating footnote in the annals of orature. The stories are etched in the collective memory of the community, waiting to be rediscovered and told. Also, this creates a vivid picture of the blurred lines between politics and spirituality.

Not only that; the tributary of the many rivers, Nqabara, Nqabarana, Shixini, Jujura and Mgadla always left me awed with exhilaration. Combined, they all composed a poetic ode to the spirit of the tributaries that flow into the majestic uMzimvubu River. The rivers are not just sources of supernatural healing but also sustain livelihoods, provide recreation, and connect some members of the community to the wealth-giving mother, uMamlambo. Also, this is where we encountered ambivalent familiars.

The confluence of rivers, a symphony of waters, flows into the Indian Ocean's embrace, creating a vibrant tapestry of life. The Nqabara Administrative Area, a kaleidoscope of natural wonders, as I knew it then, contributed to the belt or trembling mosaic of the landscape stretching from Tongaland to Pondoland. This patchwork quilt culminated from a juxtaposition of forest, grassland and woodland. The trinity of natural life created a vibrant tapestry of biodiversity, where natural abundance and spiritual significance entwine.

The highly valuable and utilised local ecological knowledge presented opportunities to gain from the abundance of natural food and cultivated medicinal plant nurseries to the almost poverty-stricken locals. This all encapsulates the acknowledgement of local ecological knowledge, which in turn highlights the importance of indigenous wisdom in harnessing the riches of nature, from food to medicine. Also, this is one of the largest geographical areas in South Africa, or holy sites, whose proximity to mainland was a sanctuary to all kinds .of life surrounding the place. It is also a radiometer within which indigenous rituals were performed by a wide range of 'indigenous healers'. Above it all, this is a testament of a complex and multifaceted world, where the natural and the supernatural coexist, and the boundaries between reality and myth blur. Amidst this complexity, life finds a way to flourish, and the landscape is reborn; a further testament to the power of nature and the human spirit to transform and transcend.

The endless gorges, a realm of mystery and encounter, where humans and ambivalent familiars intersect, morph into a lush green carpet, softening the rugged landscape and wrapping the community in an embrace of life. The village held secrets of ukuthwala, a path to wealth and power through occult means. Some individuals had succumbed to its allure, becoming conduits for the promises of the "wealth-giving mother". But at a steep price: unreasonable demands, such as celibacy or even sacrificing loved ones.

The village was a hub, attracting seekers from far and wide, including Europeans, who were drawn into the mysterious and often dark world of occult practices. The underground currents of these activities were palpable, hidden from plain sight yet pervasive in their influence. This portrays a picture of a complex, multifaceted world, where spirituality, power and greed intersect. The villagers' beliefs and practices blur the lines between reality and the unknown, revealing a rich cultural heritage steeped in mysticism and wonder.

It was a well-known fact in our village that certain people had enriched themselves through this way, or *ukuthwala*, and thus were media to offer occult promises, sometimes false, to the many disciples who arrived in this village from all corners of the country. The village had a fascinating dynamic, where wealthy men, often gaining their prosperity at the expense of women, and 'native doctors' would establish temporary dwellings along the rivers. This practice seemed to foster connections with the ambivalent familiars, blurring the lines between human and spiritual realms.

Some individuals took this further, building permanent residences at the banks of the rivers and the ocean, solidifying their bond with the natural and supernatural worlds. This proximity likely allowed them to tap into the energies and wisdom of the land, water and spirits. This scenario reveals a complex web of relationships, where gender, power, spirituality and nature intersect. The villagers' beliefs and practices highlight the significance of harmony with the environment and the unknown, and the importance of acknowledging the interconnectedness of all aspects of life.

III

The contrast between my spiritual awakening and parents' Christian beliefs created a rich tension. One day as I was playing with my mates I felt a clarion call to delve into the depths of Nqabara river. Funny nhe, my greatest king, King Hintsa kaKhawuta (Ah! Zanzolo) was slaughtered just here by Smith and his barricades. I consequently disappeared for about five days, so I am told. As my parents long suspected that my predispositions leaned more towards an ancestral calling, they never panicked. They consulted a local sangoma, gogo uNobukhosi:

"Vumani bo"

"Siyavuma"

"A journey has brought you here. It is your son. I can hear dialogues from beneath the deep pools of Nqabara. The ancestors have taken the child in order to train him and coronate him along the great line of special sangomas, *sanuses*. After five days he is going to resurface from the water. Very early in the morning, close family members and an officiating sangoma should stand at the banks of Nqabara river. Many gifts to the ancestors must be brought. This must be kept as a family secret until that time comes".

"Siyavuma".

On returning, I was welcomed by a big throng of sangomas at the banks of Nqabara river. Nobukhosi performed a multiplicity of rituals for me, culminating in the ceremonial slaughtering of a goat and a bull. Through all these events, there was a series of speeches, paused by an interlude of ceremonial traditional beer drinking, animated songs and trance induced dances, from Nobukhosi, family members and my family. The one speech delivered by one of the community elders, Jola, stood out:

> Fellow villagers, this is a rare event indeed. During the time of my childhood, I clearly remember stories of *ukuthwetyulwa*. In our day and age, we have never experienced such, especially along the death bead of our greatest king. For different reasons that I cannot mention here, the process usually aborted and many families lost their relatives, either they came back death or lost their sanity. Sikhomo, you have given birth to a god himself. It is for this reason alone that this child must not be suffocated by family rivalry or community jealous. Let him be.

The sangomas' welcome and Nobukhosi's rituals, including the sacrificial bull and goat, symbolized a profound connection to my ancestral heritage. As I immerged from the shining face of Nqabara river, the continuous beating of the African drum, the tranquilizing songs, the ululating and the spontaneous dancing all created a parallel world that pulled me more to the deep pools of the river. Both my parents were highly agitated and embarrassed by all this as they were prominent leaders in the church. They reckoned that they should quickly send me to the newly built theological centre at Salem.

I was ecstatic on the possibility of embracing a completely new world after this intense spiritual journey. Meanwhile, my parents' discomfort and eagerness to send me to the theological school at Salem revealed their desire to align me with the faith and distance me from the "heathen" practices they view as contradictory to their beliefs. My journey was not only about reconciling my ancestral calling with my personal life but also about navigating the complex web of faith, family and community expectations. The path of least resistance, or a strategic move to appease my parents while I navigated the tumultuous waters of my ancestral calling seemed to be the most palpable solution. My agreement to attend the theological school might be seen as a concession to my parents' wishes, but it also afforded me the opportunity to explore the Christian faith and its teachings more deeply:

"Mother, father, as you know, I have just returned from the river, and I have finally found my true self. For a long time now I have not been in touch with my roots as at a very young age you sent me to boarding school. Why are you sending me away again?"

Mother: "Wongalethu, we thought the seminary would be a safe place for you to learn about your faith and your newfound identity".

Wongalethu: "But I've already found my identity in the river. I have connected with my ancestors and my heritage. I don't need the seminar for that".

Father: "But what about your faith? You need guidance and training to understand your purpose"

Wongalethu: "My purpose is here, with my people. I want to share my story and inspire others to find their own way. Please, don't take me away from this again."

Mother: "We will talk with the elders, Wongalethu. But for now, the seminary is the best place for you."

Wongalethu: "But you don't understand. I've been reborn in the river. I'm not the same person I was before. Please, trust me and trust the ancestors who have guided me."

The discussion reached a *cul de sac* , and my parents' deliberations soon became an ultimatum. Within that state of vulnerability; anger; despair and utter confusion, I was finally whisked away to Salem. The trip from Nqabara to Salem seemed like the longest and boring trip in my life. The evocative landscape along the West coast seemed long dead. What haunted me was a smell of water, up to a point that I felt like I was drowning. My ears also reacted, sounding as if I am long deaf. I tried as much as possible to sleep at the back of my father's car.

As I immersed myself in the theological studies, the whispers of my ancestors and the call of Nqabara river continued to echo in my mind. The tension between these worlds persisted, and the question remained: how will I reconcile my ancestral heritage with my newfound knowledge of Christianity? The weight of my ancestral calling and the expectations of my parents' world proved too much to bear. The attempt to assimilate into the theological school's teachings only served to heighten the sense of disconnection from my true self. The memories of Nqabara river and the call from my ancestors refused to be silenced, and the tension between my two worlds reached a breaking point. Indeed, William Butler Yeats was close to the truth, "Things fall apart; the centre cannot hold".

IV

I am in the cusp of a significant chapter in my life, as I prepare to embark on my ministry. Despite the challenges I have faced, I have been entrusted with a great responsibility by the church, which has a vast reach across Southern Africa. For now, it is clear that I have many reservations. However, what matters now is that I am here, witnessing the sharp scales of this juggernaut opening and unfolding just in front of my eyes. As I navigate my duties as a theology student and probation minister, I am getting a glimpse of the magnitude of the church's influence and the weight of my future role. With few months to go before my "real" ministry begins, I am caught up in a spiral of activities both within the environs of the church and the surrounding community.

The construction of the state-of-the-art theological centre at Salem has sparked a mix of shock, curiosity and debate both within and outside the church. Engrained here in the heart of this no-man's land, it was meant to bring light to the church and surrounding communities. Cushioned by the trembling feet of iNtaba yeZono, its sullen head glittered as if a highly polished diamond had been absorbed by the red soils of ancient Zuurveld. Maybe, a huge star had fallen from the constellation of planets to this drought-stricken landscape.

This majestic and ancient panorama, where the earth itself seems to be alive and trembling, is the embodiment of a landscape as a living being that's been impacted by some extraordinary event. Intaba yeZono, which in isiXhosa directly translates as the "Mountain of Sins", whose meaning is meant to catapult a sense of cultural and historical depth which for a long time now has been lost, seems to be spilling out the secrets it had been entrusted with since the amaXhosa genocides and unrest of the early 19th century. Also, a sense of wonder and enchantment is planted, coupled with the dry landscape, adds a sense of both cosmic and material significance to the concept, as if the very fabric of the universe has been destroyed.

As per the Synod's church manual when canvassing for the establishment of the centre, the building of the cutting-edge theological centre attracted scholars, students and spiritual seekers; potentially leading to a resurgence of interest in theological studies and discussions. Although financed by a specific denomination, it was also hoped that the centre might provide a platform for inter-faith dialogue and collaboration, fostering greater understanding and co-operation among different religious communities. Also, the centre's presence could lead to increasing community engagement, with potential programmes and initiatives aimed at addressing social issues, promoting education and enhancing the local quality of life. It could also assist in generating new jobs, stimulate economic growth, and attract tourism, potentially transforming the area into a hub for religious and intellectual pursuits.

Contrary, the project faced opposition and criticism from some community members right from the onset. Prior to the construction of the centre, there had been a long-standing land dispute between a certain segment of the local community and the 'owners' of the land. The fact that this small farm area had been declared a national monument and a heritage site as a result of its direct links with the 19th century 'missionary' work in the greater Albany district presented more challenges as far as zoning is concerned. To add salt to injury, certain community members viewed it as a threat to their already dwindling churches in the area. What the governing body did not see coming was the fact that some members of the church that the centre was supposed to cater for, being the same domination as that of the centre, viewed the centre as a threat to the local hierarchy. Thus, splits became inevitable.

The fact that the state-of-the-art design and technological features of the centre could make it a landmark building, showcasing innovative and sustainable architecture, and potentially becoming a cultural icon for the region was overshadowed by these disputes and internal fights. Lastly, the possibility of the centre establishing partnerships with educational institutions and other research organisations was aborted at a very early stage

The scenario also shattered the ideology of 'partnerships' with other religious groups. Thus, as a result of this conundrum, this could no longer lead to joint projects, conferences, and publications that can have far-reaching impacts on theological scholarship and community engagement. The local churches' far reaching sight penetrated beyond this veneer of 'partnership' at quite an early stage as the church itself had a reputation of condescending behaviours such as seeking to poach members from other churches in the chase of numbers in the church roll. Of course, the common denominator was money. As accusations of corruption and money laundering were thrown at the face of the centre's board, the prospects of such illuminated dreams were very slim.

As the year marches to its abrupt closure I dramatically get detached from what I am supposed to be doing here. Instead, the allure of African realism's mystic power has captivated me, pulling me into a world of depth and meaning. By all means, I was drawn into a realm where the spiritual and material blend, where the rhythms of nature and the pulse of the ancestors resonate. African realism, a cultural and artistic movement, embraces the rich heritage and traditions of the continent. Its mystic power lies in its ability to connect us to the land, our ancestors, and the wisdom of the ages. At the present stage, it is as if I surrender. I am not sure.

IV

Due to circumstances marked by conflict and persecution, the uMzimvubu river, a majestic setting whose belly nestled the great Pondoland, became my great ancestors' home. Their roots, shrouded in a kaleidoscope of stories, with the term "Embo" being a common thread; hints at a diasporic heritage that stretches along the African coast. Following our greatest ancestor Hintsa kaKhawuta, Ah Zanzolo!, they settled here at Nqabara. The concern for their precious livestock, a vital aspect of their culture and survival, played a crucial role in their decision to settle in this picturesque landscape crowned with gushing streams, glimmering sands and lush bushes. The fact that their origins are unclear suggests a rich cultural heritage, with tales supposedly passed down through generations.

The narratives of my childhood paint a vivid picture of the complex picture of the history of my ancestors' land. The arrival of white missionaries, bearing Bibles and deceit, marked the beginning of a tumultuous chapter. Their supposed quest for spreading the word of God was tainted by hypocrisy and a hidden agenda to steal the land and exert control. During the early 19th century, King Ndamase of Western Pondoland, likely unaware of their ulterior motives, granted them permission to settle, paving the way for a gradual takeover. After the passing and planting of the king in 1876, a series of land disputes and wars ensued. The missionaries' influence was soon bolstered by colonial traders, who established stores and further solidified their grip on the land. After many genocides and betrayals, the experiment was replicated over and as they moved inland, finally settling in Zuurveld, now Makhanda.

The inevitable clashes between two worlds, one driven by a desire to claim and conquer, the other fighting to protect their ancestral land and way of life. The assegai, a symbol of traditional African weaponry, was no match for the gun, a weapon of mass destruction brought by the settlers. The collision resulted in a genocide, a dark stain on human history, where the indigenous people were brutally murdered, displaced and marginalised. The land was scorched, the culture was suppressed, and the identity of the original owners was erased. To me and many others, the memory of this genocide lives on, a testament to the enduring struggles of the original owners of the land.

The painful legacy of colonialism continues to reverberate throughout the ages, whose harbinger and social engineer was missionary work. The demotion of our kings to chiefs, the dispossessing of those whose eyes penetrated through the missionaries' (now colonisers) with both a patronising and plundering agenda (king or chief) , a deliberate attempt to erase the rich cultural heritage and sovereignty of the nation, is a wound that refuses to heal. The colonial mind-set, rooted in superiority and disdain, deemed only Queen Victoria worthy of the title "king", negating the nation's rightful leaders to a lesser status.

As I noted, this historical injustice has left an indelible mark on the collective memory of our nation, a constant reminder of the brutal suppression of our identity, autonomy, and dignity. The persecution of our kings, now chiefs, serves as a poignant symbol of the colonial era's destructive impact on indigenous culture and traditions. The nation's memory of this injustice will never fade, fuelling a resilience and determination to reclaim our heritage and restore our rightful place in history. As Nosipho Majeke (she used a pen name) once said:

> What manner of history is it that presents Tshaka, a military genius of his time, as a monster, or Hintsa, a man of pride and dignity, as a "treacherous and ungrateful savage"? What kind of British "protection" was it that robbed Ngqika and his son, Maqoma, of the land of their fathers, that rent the kingdom of Moshoeshoe with fratricidal strife and deprived a whole people of their land?"

In the South African context, I am told, the church was the handmaiden of both colonial administration and the engineers of apartheid. Of course, I seek to adopt a powerful voice in the quest for a decolonised narrative. I am seeking for words that ignite a passion for new history, one that shatters the shackles of colonialism and reclaim the stories of the marginalised. By decentring the coloniser, one seeks to restore the agency and experiences of the indigenous people, allowing their voices to echo throughout the ages.

I hope that my decolonial narrative, as Majeke concedes, will be a clarion call for a revised historical landscape, where the perspectives of the oppressed are amplified and their contributions celebrated. Through my work and many others before me, the flames of resistance and resilience are fanned, illuminating a path towards a more inclusive and truthful understanding of the past. That is the essence of my new found voice, rewriting the narrative and unshackling history from the chains of colonialism; giving voice to the silenced. The painful truth of my ancestors' history, hidden beneath the layer of colonial propaganda, yearns to be uncovered.

The bravery of King Hintsa, who refused to surrender to the English conquerors, is a testament to the resilience of my people. His tragic fate, slain at the banks of the Nqabara river, serves as a stark reminder of the colonial era's brutality. The settler's demand for land and cattle, the very lifeline of my ancestors, was more than a cruel joke, a precursor to the dispossession and displacement that followed. The humiliation, our humiliation, of the king's head being taken as a trophy, a greasy relic sent to England, is a wound that still festers. My generation, rightful heirs to this painful legacy, seeks to reclaim the truth, to restore dignity, and to honour the memory of King Hintsa and all those before and after him. The pursuit of historical accuracy, untainted by colonial bias, is a vital step towards healing and reconciliation.

The insidious tentacles of colonialism are spread all over. The offspring of missionaries, having exploited and plundered the land, strategically positioned themselves as self-proclaimed chiefs, usurping power and authority from the rightful sons of the soil; *abantwana bomgquba.* This generation of colonisers reinvented themselves as a ruling class, dominating various sectors: magistrates, police, politicians, army officers, doctors, teachers and even theologians. They manipulated the system, entrenching their control and perpetuating the oppression of indigenous people. The grip on power enabled them to distort history, cultural heritage, and even religion, forcing their own beliefs and values on the subjugated population. The value chain, once a symbol of prosperity, became a tool of oppression, spewing out colonisers in various guises, perpetuating the cycle of exploitation and cultural erasure. Such were the sinister operations of colonialism, and the resilience of my people is a testament to their unbroken spirit.

The veil of "education" and "civilisation" lifted, revealing the sinister intention of mission schools like Lovedale, Healdtown, Mountcoke, St Mathews, Salem and many others. These institutions, masquerading as bastions of learning, aimed to pacify and assimilate the native population, erasing their cultural identities and instilling a false sense of inferiority. The graduates of these schools, indoctrinated with the concepts of the "English gentlemen" and "Victorian ladies", were conditioned to abandon their heritage and embrace the colonisers' values, thereby undermining any potential resistance against their oppressors. This insidious strategy perpetuated the subjugation of native people, forcing them to relinquish their land, language, and culture. This narrative exposes the dark underbelly of colonialism *inter alia* missionary work, where education was wielded as a weapon to suppress the indigenous spirit and perpetuate the myth of white supremacy,

At this juncture I should perhaps raise a point. While the mission schools' primary intention was to pacify and assimilate, there were individuals like Nelson Mandela and many others, who, despite being products of this system, dared to challenge the colonial and consequently apartheid regimes. Their experiences and education ironically empowered them to resist and fight against the oppression they were intended to perpetuate. Mandela's journey, in particular, serves as a testament to the power of human agency and the complexity of colonialism's legacy. His exposure to the injustices of apartheid (inherited from British imperialism), combined with his education and leadership, enabled him to become a beacon of hope and a champion of equality.

V

These exceptions, though few, prove that even in the darkest systems, there are those who will resist, subvert and ultimately transform the status quo. Their stories even serve as a reminder that the human spirit can never be fully extinguished and that the pursuit of justice and equality will always find a way to emerge, even in the most unlikely of places. I myself, a product of missionary education, steeped into the very systems that sought to erase my heritage, now grappling with the disconnect between my past and my true identity. The echoes of ancient colonial North America Salem, where witchcraft was used to control and oppress, resonates with my own struggles at this seminary. My confusion is a testament to the enduring impact of colonialism, which sought to sever my roots and replace them with a fabricated narrative. Yet, here I am, seeking to reclaim my true self, navigating the labyrinth of my ancestral heritage.

For me, a soon to be conduit of missionary work and therefore a constant brainwashing of my people, one could be ensured of my irrelevancy and thus displacement from such narratives. Retrospectively, one could say my words convey a sense of nostalgia and longing for a past untouched by ravages of colonisation. However, if one can be pragmatic, this is not simply a misplaced hunger for ideologies like Negritude, a cultural and intellectual movement that celebrates the beauty and richness of Black culture, heritage and intensity. The real truth is that the stories of my real childhood serve as a reminder of the resilience and strength of my ancestors, who faced the onslaught of foreign powers with courage and determination.

As much as there were sympathisers like Mr Sunhill, I began to question the very fabric of my existence, my beliefs and my sense of self. Through a dream, the emergence of a girl from my past, a former lover perhaps, signals a significant turn in my narrative. Perhaps, the dream's vividness and the girl's centrality hint at a profound reckoning, one that will reunite me with my authentic self and my ancestral heritage. The dream, a messenger from the realm of the subconscious, compels me to return to my roots, to the place where my journey began. The poignant revelation that the girl is no longer present in my life, perhaps having moved on or passed on, adds a layer of melancholy to my journey. The dream's insistence on connecting with my past and my ancestral heritage is now tinged with a sense of longing and loss.

My return to my birthplace, prompted by the dream, becomes a symbolic gesture of reconnecting with my roots and the memories that shaped me. The absence of the girl serves as a reminder that life is fleeting, and that our connections with others are precious and ephemeral. Now is the time more than ever when I hear Jeannie Wallace

McKeown's **Lost Sonnet** reverberating throughout my blood and veins:

> I do not think I can stop loving you.
> Somehow, despite the anger and the hurt
> the love persists. Even though I grew into
> other desires, other needs, erotic
> awakening taking me by surprise
> as much as it did to you, the shock of fierce,
> to see you still raises the tempo of
> my soul's secret beat.
>
> You alone still smell like mine, not foreign
> from distant places, no trace remaining
> of my lover who was and is now gone.
> Those others I have stopped and do not miss.
> It is not my body which calls you now,
> this is not eros love, not all the time.
>
> This is a knowing, deep down deep in bone.
> You are no more mine, I not yours alone.

And so, the investigative journey unfolds. My search for answers leads me to a massive temple in Durban, a hub of spiritual and cultural significance. This grand structure, dedicated to the gods of old, seems to be holding secrets and stories that whisper tales of my ancestors. As I step into the temple's sacred space, I am enveloped by the weight of history and the presence of the divine. The air thickens with anticipation, and the whispers of my forebears grow louder, guiding me deeper into the heart of the temple.

As much as I am engrossed in this spiritual odyssey, to my surprise, I can feel and taste a certain kind of predisposition; experiencing a shift in my priorities and desires. I am no longer solely focused on my spiritual pursuits, but also craving deeper human connections and relationships:

> Returning home, trying to capture
> past connections is close to impossible.
> Moving on at your side, procrastinates all the
> possible reunions, especially that you
> have moved on, on your own. Journeys
>
> of self-discovery have explored different
> kinds of love. Its close to understandable
> that you are no longer at the same spot
> I left you, folded up like an almost creased
> grass mat behind that wind-whipped village
>
> door. Yes, rekindling the fires from the past
> seem to be very much impossible, a physical
> distance has been enacted. While rekindling
> the similar connection seems impossible,
> one way or another, we can still reach out
>
> to each other. Even if it's not the same as
> before, we can still maintain a connection
> and still dictated by the walled distance

we can still support each other, and maybe
under veiled circumstances, love each other.

Now that I know, that people grow and change
and that connections evolve into new forms
I am not giving up on us on this journey of
discovery and self enlightment, not just
physically, but also spiritually and vocational.

Mmap Nonfiction and Academic books

If you have enjoyed *THE KALEIDOSCOPE OF LIFE: Essays on Identity and Indigenous Knowledge Systems,* consider these other fine **Mmap Nonfiction and Academic books** from *Mwanaka Media and Publishing:*

Cultural Hybridity and Fixity by Andrew Nyongesa

Tintinnabulation of Literary Theory by Andrew Nyongesa

South Africa and United Nations Peacekeeping Offensive Operations by Antonio Garcia

A Case of Love and Hate by Chenjerai Mhondera

A Cat and Mouse Affair by Bruno Shora

The Scholarship Girl by Abigail George

The Gods Sleep Through It All by Wonder Guchu

PHENOMENOLOGY OF DECOLONIZING THE UNIVERSITY: Essays in the Contemporary Thoughts of Afrikology by Zvikomborero Kapuya

Africanization and Americanization Anthology Volume 1, Searching for Interracial, Interstitial, Intersectional and Interstates Meeting Spaces, Africa Vs North America by Tendai R Mwanaka

Africa, UK and Ireland: Writing Politics and Knowledge Production Vol 1 by Tendai R Mwanaka

Writing Language, Culture and Development, Africa Vs Asia Vol 1 by Tendai R Mwanaka, Wanjohi wa Makokha and Upal Deb

Zimbolicious: An Anthology of Zimbabwean Literature and Arts, Vol 3 by Tendai Mwanaka

Drawing Without Licence by Tendai R Mwanaka

Writing Grandmothers/ Escribiendo sobre nuestras raíces: Africa Vs Latin America Vol 2 by Tendai R Mwanaka and Felix Rodriguez

Nationalism: (Mis)Understanding Donald Trump's Capitalism, Racism, Global Politics, International Trade and Media Wars, Africa Vs North America Vol 2 by Tendai R Mwanaka

It Is Not About Me: Diaries 2010-2011 by Tendai Rinos Mwanaka

Chitungwiza Mushamukuru: An Anthology from Zimbabwe's Biggest Ghetto Town by Tendai Rinos Mwanaka

The Day and the Dweller: A Study of the Emerald Tablets by Jonathan Thompson

Zimbolicious Anthology Vol 4: An Anthology of Zimbabwean Literature and Arts by Tendai Rinos Mwanaka and Jabulani Mzinyathi

Parks and Recreation by Abigail George

FAMILY LAW AND POLITICS WITH BIOLOGY AND ROYALTY IN AFRICA AND NORTH AMERICA by Peter Ateh-Afec Fossungu

Writing Robotics, Africa Vs Asia, Vol 2 by Tendai Rinos Mwanaka

Zimbolicious Anthology Vol 5: An Anthology of Zimbabwean Literature and Arts by Tendai R. Mwanaka

Love Notes: Everything is Love, An Anthology of Indigenous Languages of Africa and East Europe by Tendai R Mwanaka

Zimbolicious Anthology Vol 6: An Anthology of Zimbabwean Literature and Arts by Tendai R. Mwanaka and Chenjerai Mhondera

BATTLING LANGUAGE RIGHTS GOVERNANCE IN AFRICA: SWISSELGIANISM, UBACKISM, AND THE AMBAZONIA-CAMEROUN WAR by Peter Ateh-Afec Fossungu

Otherness and Pathology: The Fragmented Self and Madness in Contemporary African Fiction by Andrew Nyongesa

Zimbabwe: The Urgency of Now by Tendai Rinos Mwanaka

Zimbabwe: The Blame Game, Recollected essays and Non-fictions by Tendai Rinos Mwanaka

The Trick is to Keep Breathing: Covid 19 Stories From African and North American Writers, Vol 3 by Tendai Rinos Mwanaka

Recentring Mother Earth by Andrew Nyongesa

Zimbabwe: Beyond Robert Mugabe by Tendai Rinos Mwanaka

Language, Thought, Art and Existence: New and Recollected Essays and Non Fictions by Tendai Rinos Mwanaka

Experimental Writing, Africa Vs Latin America Vol 1 by Tendai Rinos Mwanaka and Ricardo Felix Rodriguez

Fixing Earth Anthology: An anthology of Africa, UK and Ireland Writers, Vol 2 by Tendai Rinos Mwanaka

Africa Must Deal with Blats for Its True Decolonisation: Unclothed Truth about Internalised Internal Colonialism by Nkwazi N. Mhango

ROYAL BURIAL AND ENTHRONEMENT IN AMBAZONIA: INTERROGATING THE RELEVANCE OF POSTCOLONIAL EDUCATION IN AFRICA by Peter Ateh-Afec Fossungu

SCHOOL BASED HIV EDUCATION AFFECTING GIRLS IN SELECTED COUNTRIES IN SUB SAHARAN AFRICA by Ivainesu Charmaine Musa

HIV AND AIDS IN ZIMBABWE: A REVIEW ON THE RELATIONSHIP BETWEEN PERCEPTION OF MASCULINITY AMONGST UNMARRIED YOUNG MEN AND THEIR SEXUAL BEHAVIORS by Lucas Kudakwashe Muvhiringi

AFRICA'S CONTEMPORARY FOOD INSECURITY: SELF-INFLICTED WOUNDS THROUGH MODERN VENI VIDI VICI AND LAND GRABBING by Nkwazi Mhango

I Can't Breathe and other Essays by Zvikomborero Kapuya

Ayabacholization Classroom In My Life: The Longest Shortcut To University Education by Peter Ateh-Afec Fossungu

Gathering Evidence by Tendai Rinos Mwanaka

Best New African poets 10th anniversary: Interviews and Reviews by Tendai Rinos Mwanaka

In the footsteps of a Bipolar Life by Ambrose Cato George and Abigail George

No Business Like Love Business by Peter Atec-Afec Fossungu

RE-ENGINEERING UNDER-EXPLORED RENEWABLE ENERGY by Blessing Barnet Chiniko

Manifestations of trauma in the post-2000 Zimbabwean Literature by Nyarai Maria Kanyemba

Donald Trump's Second Coming: Is Democracy, Dead, Dying or Alive by Tendai Rinos Mwanaka

HISTORY IN HISTORY OF AMBAZONIA RESISTENCE by Peter Afec-Ateh Fossungu

Zimbolicious 10th Anniversary Anthology: New and Collected Non-fictions by Tendai Rinos Mwanaka

Letters to Dariah by Rumbi Chen

Upcoming books

https://facebook.com/MwanakaMediaAndPublishing

www.ingramcontent.com/pod-product-compliance
Lightning Source LLC
Chambersburg PA
CBHW070348270326
41926CB00017B/4036